# GRAPHIC DESIGN SOURCE BOOK

*Fortune magazine, cover by Garretto, US, 1932.*

# GRAPHIC DESIGN SOURCE BOOK

LIZ McQUISTON ▪ BARRY KITTS

Macdonald Orbis

A *Macdonald Orbis* **BOOK**

Copyright © 1987 Quarto Publishing plc

First published in Great Britain in 1987
by Macdonald Orbis
London and Sydney

A member of BPCC plc

British Library Cataloguing in Publication Data

McQuiston, Liz
The graphic design sourcebook.
1. Commercial art – history – 20th century
I. Title  II. Kitts, Barry
741.6'09'04     NC998

ISBN 0-356-14809-2

This book was designed and produced by
Quarto Publishing plc
The Old Brewery, 6 Blundell Street,
London N7 9BH

**Senior Editor** Lorraine Dickey
**Art Editors** Iona McGlashan, Gill Elsbury

**Editors** Lisa Hardy, Ricki Ostrov, Henrietta Wilkinson
**Production Editor** Joanna Bradshaw

**Designers** Philip Chidlow, Ralph Pitchford

**Picture Researcher** Lucy Bullivant

**Art Director** Moira Clinch
**Editorial Director** Carolyn King

Typeset by Text Filmsetters and Aptimage Ltd
Manufactured in Hong Kong by Regent Publishing Services Ltd
Printed by Leefung-Asco Printers Ltd, Hong Kong

| The authors would like to thank the following specialist contributors: | F.H.K. Henrion Sean Perkins Richard Goust Linda Reynolds |
| --- | --- |

# THE AUTHORS

# INTRODUCTION BY...

Liz McQuiston refers to herself as an anglicized American, having been a resident of Great Britain since 1972. She has a Master's degree in Graphic Design from the Royal College of Art, and for the past ten years has divided her professional life between graphic design teaching and practice.

Barry Kitts was born in Bath and grew up in London. He commenced his art education at Kingston School of Art before studying painting and graphic design at Wimbledon School of Art. He worked in the Department of Art at the Imperial War Museum 1970-76. In 1975 he was co-art director for Stuart Cooper's award-winning film *Overlord*.

At present he is a Visiting Lecturer on the postgraduate course in Design and Media Technology at the London College of Printing. He also teaches information design at Ravensbourne College of Design and Communication.

F.H.K. Henrion, OBE, RDI, PPSIA, AGI is one of this century's most influential designers. Having trained as a poster, textile and graphic designer in Paris in the mid 1930s, he worked in advertising and publishing (both books and magazines). During the Second World War, his consultative work on exhibitions and posters for both the UK and US government information offices was widely acclaimed. In addition, he is highly respected for his corporate identity designs; he worked for KLM (Royal Dutch Airlines) for 25 years until 1984 as well as for the General Post Office (now British Telecom) during the 1960s. He has taught and lectured at over 20 universities worldwide and at the Royal College of Art, London.

# CONTENTS

# INTRODUCTION

T his book fills a much needed gap in the scant literature on graphic design and its history, going some considerable way towards reinforcing the body of knowledge on which every profession must be built. In the 90-year period it covers, enormous changes have taken place — changes which could not have been dreamed of in the early years of this century. Gone are the days of the 'commercial artist', that rather derogatory term in common use up to at least 1940. Graphic designers are now members of a high-status profession — often government-sponsored, media-fêted and wealthy. Design is a growth industry, and the more talented art-school graduates are in the happy position of finding themselves in a seller's market.

But it is interesting to reflect that, although the words 'graphic' and 'design' are so much part of our everday vocabulary, few people really know the extent to which design affects us or understand what it involves. We may notice, when reaching for a can or a package from the supermarket shelf, that this one looks more attractive than the similar product next to it, but we know little of the skill, judgement and training that have contributed to its special appearance. The fact is that almost every man-made thing around us is *designed*, and because we live in a largely man-made environment, designers can be seen as contributing to the quality of life.

This comprehensive survey of design and designers through the century supports such a view, in both text and illustrations. It will enable consumers (which means all of us) to look at graphic designers and their recent history with more respect and understanding, so that, one hopes, the latter will improve their performance and the former may become either more sympathetic clients or at least better-informed and enlightened consumers.

During its voyage through almost a century, the book charts the people and their work; the events and the media, and the context in which it all came about, all in chronological and geographical sequence. Many historians find it comfortable to write about the dead, who cannot answer back or refute a viewpoint stated by the author, but here Liz and Barry bring their story right into the present, running the risk of disagreement from their subjects. I myself, invited to write this introduction, am a survivor of the very events being dealt with — an active participant for 50 years and a witness to the significant evolution from 'commercial artist' to 'graphic designer' and more recently to 'visual communicator'.

In my own career I have tried to combine practice, organization and teaching, and in both my professional capacity and as a member of the public I have welcomed a publication which adds substantially to the understanding of a profession that I have seen develop from easel to drawing board to computer console; from one-man freelance efforts to design offices of four hundred people or more; from pawnbroker finance to public companies with accountants and financial directors.

But it should always be borne in mind that, however sophisticated the technology may become and however large the fees, the important qualities in graphic design are the same as they have always been — and they come from the eye and the intellect, from the head and from the heart. A successful visual communicator must always be able to communicate, and thus must possess above all the quality of empathy, the capacity to understand those to whom the message is addressed. Good graphic design should be for everyone, not just for its initiator.

*F.H.K. Henrion*
*June 1987*

*'Etoile du Nord', A.M. Cassandre, France, 1927.*

# CHAPTER · ONE
# 1900
## TO
# 1929

# INTRODUCTION

Graphic design in the modern sense was born in the early decades of this century, out of the spirit of innovation and change. The turn of the century brought new attitudes and for the Modernists graphic design and printing represented the futuristic marriage of art and industry.

The innovators responsible for its early development were often 'universal' artists who crossed disciplines freely, designing not only graphic material but also industrial products, exhibitions, buildings or theatre sets, and often involved in the fine arts or writing. It is not surprising that graphic design continued to develop over the years as a hybrid field, borrowing principles and methods from mathematics, engineering and psychology for its problem-solving activities, while still retaining a spiritual and emotional connection with fine art. (This hybrid character is a vital creative quality which keeps the boundaries of the field permanently 'fuzzy'.)

The industrial and technological advances taking place in Europe, Britain and America at the turn of the century provided a strong basis for the so-called union of art and industry, although it played a very different role in each of these societies. In Europe, revolutionary art movements found an important mode of expression in graphic design and typography, and in so doing created a new visual vocabulary that is still influential today. In America, advertising was already firmly linked with commerce and industry, and advertising agencies flourished while developing the art of persuasion. Britain, in the aftermath of the Arts and Crafts Movement's backlash against industrialized society, put graphic art and design to work in the service of the public.

During World War I the modern poster, which had been established as a successful persuasive tool for commercial advertising and a popular art form, was exploited by governments for use on the public and played a significant role in sustaining one of the bloodiest wars in human history. Finally two late nineteenth century art movements helped to prepare the ground for the new age of Modernism: Art Nouveau and The Arts and Crafts Movement.

Art Nouveau was the name attributed to a decorative style characterized by floral motifs, organic forms and fluid, curved lines. Internationally it manifested itself mainly in the applied arts, but also found its way into the graphic and fine arts. In the 1890s great French masters such as Jules Chéret, Toulouse-Lautrec and Pierre Bonnard transformed the poster into a work of art, which allowed for the development of the modern advertising poster after the turn of the century. Other strong representatives of the movement included Czech poster artist Alphonse Mucha, British illustrator Aubrey Beardsley and German artist, architect and designer Peter Behrens. In addition, the typography of Art Nouveau with its flowing asymmetry, floral motifs and borders, and decorative display typefaces

*Loie Fuller at the Folies Bergère, poster, Jules Cheret, France, 1897.*

provided a lingering influence up until the 1920s. Art Nouveau passed on the essential qualities of freedom and vitality, so strongly shown in its graphic work, to the Modern Movement.

The British-based Arts and Crafts Movement, led by the socialist William Morris, was essentially a reaction against nineteenth century industrialization. Its driving force was a reverence for craftsmanship, traditional production methods and the use of natural materials. A broad-based movement that included architects, artists, writers, designers and philosophers, its inspirations and ideas stemmed from Medievalism and its imagery dwelled in nature and the use of plant, bird and animal forms. The movement prompted a surge of private presses including Morris's own Kelmscott Press. Morris himself produced three Gothic-inspired typefaces, two of which are highly readable black-letter types. The Modern Movement, and in particular the Bauhaus, borrowed its emphasis on craft skills and the value of understanding and handling materials from the Arts and Crafts Movement.

### Germany

The new approach to industrialization, involving mass manufacture and standardization, was adopted enthusiastically in Germany. The Deutsche Werkbund was formed in 1907, an organization intended to pressure the union of art and industry. It encouraged design in manufacturing, and promoted improvements in the design and quality of German products to both German manufacturers and the general public.

Much of Europe's best type and print technology was found in Germany at this time, and high standards of book

*Items from AEG corporate identity, Peter Behrens, Germany, c.1908.*

A well-known Werkbund member was the Berlin architect and designer Peter Behrens, renowned as the world's first major industrial designer and the founding father of corporate identity – due to his design of the AEG (General Electric) corporate scheme. His work for AEG (c. 1907) included the famous redesign of the AEG factory; graphics such as catalogues, advertisements, posters, packaging and stationery; electrical appliances and other products. Interestingly, Behrens' earlier work was heavily embedded in the Art Nouveau movement. The AEG scheme involved a distinct transfer to the new industrial aesthetic and functionalism, most pronounced in his product designs. His graphic work for AEG however still retained Art Nouveau influences. Behrens was a perfect example of the 'universal artist' and operated comfortably as an architect, industrial designer, graphic designer, typographer and poster artist!

production were achieved in the publishing centres of Leipzig and Berlin. A particular promoter of good book design was the publishing firm Insel-Verlag of Leipzig. In 1905 their series of octavo-sized pocket books of German classics created a new notion of 'the popular book' – precursors of the popular classics produced in paperback by Britain's Penguin Books in the 1930s. Despite two World Wars Insel-Verlag still publishes today in West Germany.

Leading German typographers of the period designed typefaces for the Stempel, Bauer and Klingspor type foundries. F. W. Kleukens designed for Stempel, Walter Tiemann and E. R. Weiss designed for Bauer, and Klingspor's designers included Peter Behrens, Otto Eckmann and Rudolf Koch. A glance through the early 1900s catalogues for Klingspor reveals the continued influence of Art Nouveau, coupled with a highly pragmatic and commercial approach to graphic design – for example, selling off-the-peg letterheads and trade symbols to professional users.

Germany's commercial approach to graphics extended to poster art. Posters for consumer products were designed by first class commercial artists, who combined art with advertising techniques. The professional poster artists of this period were internationally admired and imitated, and their posters were reproduced as popular art prints and collected by the public. Poster artists Ludwig Hohlwein and Lucian Bernhard attained world standing, and others included Julius Klinger, Paul Scheurich, Julius Gipkens, Ernst Deutsch, Hans Rudi Erdt, Jo Steiner, Louis Oppenheim, Thomas Theodor Heine (political posters), Bruno Paul, E. R. Weiss, Fritz Helmut Ehmcke and Peter Behrens. The work of commercial cartoonists and illustrators also appeared in magazines such as *Simplicissimus*, the renowned weekly of political satire (1896-1933). Thomas Theodor Heine, co-founder and contributor to the magazine, was well-known for his bulldog poster, symbol of the magazine and its aggressive, satirical character.

During World War I, designs for war posters were often chosen through competitions. Design competitions were already a well established convention in Germany and the German Poster Society (Verein der Plakatfreunde) organized war poster competitions which offered prize money for winning designs, and attracted entries from the leading professionals.

The posters themselves depicted an idealistic form of patriotism – the individual courage and sacrifice of the soldier-hero. Emphasis was on masculine values and the military contribution to the war. Allegorical figures were rarely used, women rarely appeared nor did ordinary civilians as in British and American posters. They also made consistent use of an important psychological device (which became more exaggerated in later Nazi posters) – the representation of figures from a low viewpoint, increasing their power to intimidate by forcing the viewer to look up at the images.

*Design for Job cigarette papers, Alphonse Mucha, France, 1896.*

*Joseph Binder, industry exhibition poster, Germany, 1922.*

## The Art Movements

In the midst of Europe's pre-war industrialization and commercialism, an intellectual upheaval occurred. Rejection of the decadence of old Europe, its traditions and social order took explosive form in a series of art movements which shattered existing art and design conventions and proposed a new vision of an industrial world. Graphic design and typography became instruments of expression for the art movements – carriers of group manifestoes, personal theories and obsessions which were often published by the artists themselves. In the hands of artists, philosophers and fanatics, a totally new visual language was created for graphic design over a twenty-year period of innovation (1910-1930).

The art movements of this period are thoroughly documented in other publications and are best appreciated when explored in depth. This section only provides a brief outline of the movements and personalities involved as a prompt for further reading.

Futurism, a movement originating in pre-war Italy, provided the revolutionary break with the past by condemning bourgeois society, traditions and sentimentalism – and embracing disorder, chaos and the modern life. It glorified the beauties of speed, movement and the machine, and welcomed power, violence and the heightened experience of war. The Manifesto of Futurism, written by the poet and writer F. T. Marinetti, was published in the French newspaper *Le Figaro* in 1909. Although Futurism began as a literary movement, it was quickly adopted by visual artists. It spread across Europe and established itself in England (in the form of the Vorticist Movement) and Russia. It spread not only across countries, thereby making the Modern Movement international, but also across disciplines, involving artists, designers and architects.

In 1915 the Russian Futurist painter Kasimir Malevich founded Suprematism, with abstract paintings consisting of simple geometric shapes. Another Russian movement, Constructivism, involved a loose group of artists and designers (such as Alexander Rodchenko, El Lissitzky and Vladimir Tatlin) who applied Suprematist forms to 'real work' in industrial design, textiles, theatre sets, furniture and posters. When the Bolshevik Revolution took place in 1917, both of these avant garde movements worked in the service of the revolution and upheld its ideals of technological progress and social equality. Artists and designers put their ideas and products to use directly in the 'construction' of the new society.

Yet another movement brewed in Switzerland. In 1916 Dadaism was born, out of disgust for the stupidity and slaughter of World War I. Pioneered by Hans Arp, Hugo Ball and Tristan Tzara, it used shock tactics and ridicule to protest against the war, society, religion, art and all established values. It spread quickly to other countries, and Dada groups were soon found in New York, Paris, and Berlin.

# INTRODUCTION

Dada's passionate rejection of just-about-everything demanded powerful new communication methods which resulted in the use of new forms of poetry, and new visual techniques such as collage and photomontage. Kurt Schwitters visually led the way with his *Merz*-collages, which were compositions of everyday rubbish and ephemera. John Heartfield, George Grosz, Raoul Hausmann and Hannah Höch experimented with photomontage in Berlin, as did Alexander Rodchenko in Moscow. The technique later became an important tool for political propaganda by both Rodchenko and Heartfield, and also found innovative use in advertising through Piet Zwart and Paul Schuitema in Holland. The Dada experiments of this era, particularly in typography, collage and photomontage, revolutionized graphic communication and are still considered to have a heavy influence on present-day graphic designers. The Dada use of collage was carried even further by Surrealism, an offshoot of Dada which began in Paris (1924) and developed into an international movement in the 1930s.

Futurism, Suprematism, Constructivism, De Stijl and Dadaism all operated with different philosophies and principles, but were in no way isolated from each other. The members of the different movements often communicated and visited each other to lecture or conduct work, and even collaborated on projects. In the early 1920s Berlin was the rising intellectual centre of Europe and also provided a connecting point for the art movements. Of particular importance was the Russian Constructivist Exhibition held in Berlin in 1922, in which Constructivist art and artists were exhibited as a major movement outside of Russia for the first time. Through this exhibition, Constructivism made a heavy impact on the prevailing art and design scene. And in the meantime, Berlin had acquired two new residents – El Lissitsky from Russia and the Hungarian Moholy-Nagy, while the De Stijl leader Van Doesburg visited frequently.

From 1921 to 1924 El Lissitzky took advantage of Berlin's sophisticated printing facilities and produced a large quantity of superb typographic work. He also acted as the connecting link between the different movements, for he was in contact with many of the leading personalities and was involved in the important art publications of the period – the Constructivist magazine *Veshch*, the Dadaist journal *Merz*, and the Dutch journal *De Stijl*.

Again in Holland, Piet Zwart and Paul Schuitema (working separately) were applying the principles of Constructivism and De Stijl to commercial advertising. Pioneers of photomontage and radical masters of the new typography, they managed to combine functionalism with a strong sense of optimisim. Zwart was the more playful of the two, visually speaking. Despite working in the heavy black and primary colours of De Stijl, his typography displays a spirit of fun and movement not easily matched, even in the 1980s.

Meanwhile in Weimar Germany, the Modern Movement's most crucial educational exercise was underway. In

At the same time, the Modern Movement appeared in Holland in the form of De Stijl, a movement which included painters, sculptors, writers and architects. Its main vehicle was a journal called *De Stijl*, which first appeared in 1917, and it adopted a strict purist view that harmony was achieved through minimal elements – horizontal and vertical lines (no curves or diagonals); the non-colours of black, white and grey; and the primary colours of red, blue and yellow. Theo van Doesburg and Piet Mondrian acted as the movement's main theorists, and its principles were most clearly expressed through the minimalist paintings of Mondrian and the buildings and furniture designs of Gerrit Rietveld.

1919 Walter Gropius had established the Bauhaus School, seeking to break down the barriers between artist, architect, craftsman and industry – another promotion of the marriage of art and industry. Students were educated in the basic principles of design and also in craft skills, and the idea of designers and craftsmen working side by side was fundamental to the Bauhaus. An important feature of the educational structure was the six-month Preliminary Course of basic design studies, which was considered to be the foundation of the Bauhaus study programme. Another important aspect was that students received craft training in workshops as an integral part of their study, in order to develop an understanding of industry, materials, and modern production problems.

The school's early development was shaky, largely due to difficulties surrounding the Preliminary Course run by Johannes Itten. (It was later taken over by Moholy-Nagy and Albers.) Around 1921 Van Doesburg moved to Weimar and through peripheral talks and sessions held in his own home, heavily influenced Bauhaus students and staff with the theories of De Stijl. In 1922 a stronger direction resulted from the arrival of new staff to the school – Laszlo Moholy-Nagy (who quickly became one of the most influential teachers), Paul Klee and Wassily Kandinsky. Moholy-Nagy involved himself and his students in experimentation with photography and typography, but graphic design as such

Lissitzky lectured in Poland during this period and made a great impression on Henryk Berlewi. Berlewi immediately began working on experiments in mechanical constructivism or 'Mechano-facture', creating graphic compositions of simple geometrical and typographical elements which were mechanically reproducible. In 1924 Berlewi published his theory, 'Mechano-facture' and, with two other members of the Polish avant garde, opened an advertising agency in Warsaw called Reklama Mechano – devoted to applying the principles of 'Mechano-facture' to advertising.

was not on the Bauhaus curriculum.

In 1925 the school moved to the small town of Dessau and the staff grew to include Herbert Bayer, Josef Albers, Marcel Breuer and Joost Schmidt. Graphic design was now added to the curriculum, and Herbert Bayer was made head of the newly-named Department of Typography and Advertising Design. Bayer taught typography along strict Constructivist lines, was a heavy advocate of sans serif types and strongly favoured use of a single alphabet. In 1925 the Bauhaus abandoned the use of capital letters, and designs were produced by Joost Schmidt and Herbert Bayer for single alphabets constructed from limited geometric shapes. These were possible candidates for a universal 'ideal' alphabet, and the ultimate in De Stijl minimalism. (The geometric alphabets produced by Schmidt and Bayer remained essentially drawing board exercises. However Futura, a geometric sans serif typeface designed by Paul Renner in Munich was issued in 1927 and became one of the most successful typefaces developed from the 'new typography'.)

It was during this Dessau period that the Bauhaus reached maturity and produced its best work, until Gropius retired in 1928. The school moved to Berlin in 1930 and was closed by the Nazis in 1933, bringing Modernism in Germany to an abrupt halt. The Bauhaus remains a major influence in art and design history and education, for the personalities involved spread Bauhaus concepts around the world, and down through generations of students.

It follows that the new machine age should proclaim a new typography with which to express itself. *Die Neue Typographie* (The New Typography) was a product of the Modern Movement. It employed strict functionalism, sans serif typefaces (glorified because they were stripped of all decoration) and asymmetric layout – considered to be more dynamic than other arrangements, and more sympathetic to the nature of language (as opposed to forcing it into a predetermined shape).

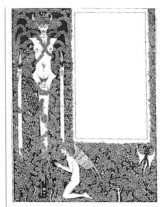

*'Salome' by Oscar Wilde, Aubrey Beardsley, Britain, 1894.*

The New Typography was practised by the art movements and was central to the experiments of the Bauhaus, but it was the typographer Jan Tschichold who placed the Modernist theories into a form which could be related to everyday printing. In his writing on modern typography he constructed a very dogmatic method which would allow printers and compositors to apply asymmetric typography to their daily work. He was also a skilled practitioner and produced a vast range of typographic work, making a particularly valuable contribution in the area of book design. In 1928 he published the book *Die Neue Typographie*, and in 1933 was forced by the Nazis to flee to Switzerland for creating 'un-German' typography.

## Britain

Britain in the early 1900s was still very much under the lingering influences of William Morris and the Arts and Crafts Movement. It did not take on board the Modern Movement and its industrial ethic as Europe did. Craftsmanship was still held supreme.

Poster design flourished at the turn of the century in the hands of the Beggarstaff Brothers, J. W. Simpson, John Hassall, Aubrey Beardsley, Charles Rennie Mackintosh, Dudley Hardy, Cecil Aldin and others. Aubrey Beardsley and Charles Rennie Mackintosh were particularly strong representatives of English Art Nouveau. The Beggarstaff Brothers (a pseudonym for William Nicholson and James Pryde) set a new trend of stylized simplicity in poster design and are said to have been a major influence on Ludwig Hohlwein, the great German poster artist.

Posters were not however considered works of art as in Germany, and were often created for advertising products such as food and to promote public utilities, such as transport. In the 1920s Frank Pick, in charge of London Transport's corporate style, commissioned well-known artists and designers for posters and other projects. This included the use of Edward Johnston's sans serif typeface as part of the new corporate identity scheme for the London Underground.

With the outbreak of World War I, Britain followed other countries in speaking to its public through war posters. The British war poster artists were a mixed bag of magazine illustrators, commercial poster artists such as John Hassall, well-known fine artists such as Frank Brangwyn, and many others who were simply draftsmen employed by the printing firms publishing the posters. War posters were commissioned by the War Propaganda Bureau and the Parliamentary Recruiting Committee (both government organizations), as well as private companies such as the London Electric Railways Company.

Unlike other countries, the majority of war posters issued in Britain were recruitment posters. Whereas other countries in Europe enforced compulsory military service, Britain alone relied on a volunteer army until it finally

In Holland Hendrik Werkman was also experimenting with the use of printers materials and letterforms as the components of graphic compositions. Werkman's 'druksels' (prints), however, were definitely not aimed at reproduction. They were often printed with forms he came across in his immediate surroundings (anything that came to hand), making a highly personal form of print-collage. The emotional quality of his prints placed Werkman outside of De Stijl and Constructivism, although he was in contact with and was influenced by both. He produced his own publication *The Next Call* (ten issues, starting in 1923) which contained typographical experiments and texts written by himself and sent them all over the world to friends or in exchange for other avant garde journals, thereby keeping in touch with the international scene.

# INTRODUCTION

adopted conscription in 1916. The most successful recruitment poster was Alfred Leete's poster of Lord Kitchener pointing an accusing finger at the public and declaring 'Your country needs YOU'.

Artistically speaking Britain's war posters were generally undistinguished and often ·technically poor, especially those emanating from printers' art departments. However, they could also be said to have pioneered new heights of moral blackmail. The civilian public was constantly battered with shaming implications of cowardice, sense of duty, loss of honour – often using women and children to make the point hit home. The 'atrocity' propaganda directed against the Germans by both Britain and America often reached hysteria pitch.

The period from 1895-1920 also saw the emergence of large newspaper empires and the beginning of Fleet Street, with the *Morning Post* and Lord Northcliff's *Daily Mail*. Both newspapers and magazines were highly influential media during World War I, and joined in the recruitment drive. (The *London Opinion* magazine, for example, published the Lord Kitchener poster.) The power of the empires lasted until the 1920s and was then demolished with the establishment of the British Broadcasting Corporation (BBC) in 1927.

## The United States

American commercial entrepreneurialism at the turn of the century was heavily based on advertising linked with industry (the home market). Press advertising, mail order catalogues and travelling salesmanship were all directed at the American consumer.

Advertising agencies had emerged in America as early as the 1840s. They originally started as brokers of 'white space' in newspapers (they would buy space in newspapers and then re-sell it to manufacturers). The next step was selling space, plus an advert to go with it. By the 1900s, commercial advertising agencies were firmly established along with rapidly developing techniques of persuasion.

Three of America's oldest space brokerage houses grew to become, at this point in time, its largest agencies: J. Walter Thompson, founded in New York in 1864, N. W. Ayer, founded in Philadelphia in 1869 and Lord & Thomas, founded in Chicago in 1873 and later named Foote, Cone & Belding. (All three are still leaders in the field today.) Although advertising agencies ·proliferated all over the country, Chicago and New York City were the major centres. New York City was the gateway to Europe and the Madison Avenue agencies boasted sophistication and internationalism, close to the nation's financial core on Wall Street. Chicago was seen as the geographic, industrial and transport centre of the nation – the heartbeat of the home market, so to speak.

Type technology made great advances in America around the turn of the century. After fire destroyed their

**BASKE**
**GARA**
**GILL SA**
**BEMB**

Britain can also claim important developments in type technology and design during this era, through the work of the Lanston Monotype Company. The Monotype composing machine was originally invented in America in 1887, but due to lack of finance the business was taken over by a British syndicate and by 1900 manufacturing had been transferred to England. The composing machine was developed to a high level of sophistication and the company embarked on a 'golden era' of prosperity and world recognition. Many of its most popular typefaces were cut in the 1920s, including Baskerville, Garamond, Grotesque 215/216 (copies of German grotesques), Gill Sans, Bembo, Perpetua and Goudy (Old Style and Modern). Equally important, the Lanston Monotype Corporation employed some of the leading type 'personalities' of this period – Frank Hinman Pierpont, manufacturing manager; Stanley Morison and Beatrice Warde, typographical advisers and Eric Gill, type designer. In 1931 the company's name was changed to The Monotype Corporation, as it is still known today.

equipment and premises and necessitated starting from 'scratch', the Chicago typefounders Marder, Luse and Company began to produce types on point bodies (c. 1878). In 1886 the United States Type Founders Association assigned a committee to report on the new point system. As a result of their report, the American point system (based on 12 points equalling one pica) was introduced in the United States and by 1898 had become the standard system of measurement used by both British and American printers and typefounders. (Hence the Anglo-American point system.)

In the 1880s Linotype machines, with direct entry keyboards and line casting, revolutionized text setting – particularly for newspapers. The Lanston Monotype Company appeared in the 1890s with the Monotype composing machine, however by 1897 it had sold out to a British syndicate and was thereafter developed in Britain.

**Cooper**
**Caled**
**Goudy**

Three great masters of letter design were associated with Chicago during this period: Oswald (Oz) Cooper, Frederic Goudy and William A. Dwiggins. Oswald Cooper was co-founder of Bertsch & Cooper, which offered a lettering, layout and typesetting service to the advertising and newspaper industries. His lettering for Packard Motor Car Company was reproduced in type by American Typefounders (ATF) in 1913, and from 1920-1928 he designed the Cooper Black family of typefaces. Frederic Goudy produced many typefaces, often based on historic models, including the popular Goudy and Kennerley typefaces. William A. Dwiggins was a student of Goudy and a renowned book designer who later (in 1938) designed the popular American book face Caledonia.

Although cruder in many ways, Linotype machines were developed more rapidly than Monotype and quickly became the largest selling models in the newspaper world. Typefounding as an industry suffered as a result of the new technology, although it was still needed for display setting. Seeking strength in numbers, typefounding companies banded together to form the American Typefounders (ATF), which was responsible for cutting many popular faces such as Goudy Oldstyle, Century, Jenson, Franklin Gothic and News Gothic.

Two great American scholars of typography and printing were also at work during this period. Theodore Low De Vinne (the De Vinne Press, New York) was one of the leading printers and publishers of his time, as well as a highly respected writer on early printing and printing types. He printed the *Century Magazine* and in 1895/6 commissioned the Century series of typefaces for use in the magazine – one of the most influential of modern typeface designs. De Vinne's successor was Daniel Berkeley Updike, another great scholar who produced the classic two-volume study *Printing Types: Their History, Forms and Use (A Study in Survivals)*. The first edition was printed in 1922.

From 1914 to 1917 public opinion was strongly against entering the war in Europe. When the US finally declared war against Germany in 1917, the government had to unite the country solidly behind the war effort and posters were seen as the chief means of mobilizing public enthusiasm (radio and film were still too young). The Committee on Public Information (CPI) was formed as the central co-ordinating agency for all United States propaganda. The Division of Pictorial Publicity of the CPI was run by illustrator Charles Dana Gibson (of 'Gibson Girl' fame) and international graphic artist Joseph Pennell, and produced posters on demand for government departments.

The Division of Pictorial Publicity produced some 700

*US Navy recruiting poster, Howard Chandler Christy, US, 1917.*

poster designs for over 50 individual agencies (special groups) and the posters were often produced in different cities, by different printers. The quantities were high – posters were usually printed in editions of 10,000 up to one million copies each. Posters for national campaigns were produced on a massive scale. For the First Liberty Loan, 2 million were printed; for the Second, 5 million printed; for the Third, 9 million printed. More posters were produced in the United States than anywhere else in the world, and were mainly the work of popular artists (illustrators for books and popular magazines) and art academies. The Chicago Academy of Fine Arts, for example, and other schools ran poster competitions and war poster painting classes.

American war posters were largely dependent on realistic representations of human figures, either appealing to the audience or accusing them. Uncle Sam often appeared and women were an important part of the poster imagery, providing sex appeal, glamour, and often shown in the allegorical forms of Columbia or the Statue of Liberty (unlike the masculinity of the German posters).

Not surprisingly, a division existed between war poster art and avant garde art. The American avant garde artists and intellectuals who followed the new European movements (such as Futurism) were not involved in making war posters and like their European counterparts found the concept of war disillusioning and frightening. The popular artists, that is poster makers, preferred to see themselves as working for the state and serving the people, and criticized the avant garde artists for producing 'art for art's sake'.

The American economy boomed through the 1920s until The Wall Street Crash took place on 24 October 1929 ('Black Friday') and set off a world economic crisis. The Depression that followed in 1930s America provided a heavy contrast to the escapism and glamour found in 'Hollywood Style' and the extravagant fantasy productions of Broadway.

# PACKAGING

**1** *'I'm Cook's Assistant → Like OXO', point of sale card, Britain, c.1930.* **2** *Cadbury's Dairy Milk chocolate, display card, Britain, c.1900.* **3** *Grape Nuts packaging, Britain, c.1915.* **4** *Mayfair chocolates and Bristows talc de luxe packaging, Britain, c.1905.*

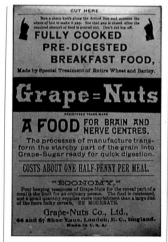

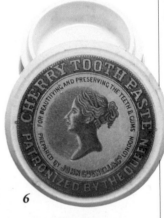

**5**

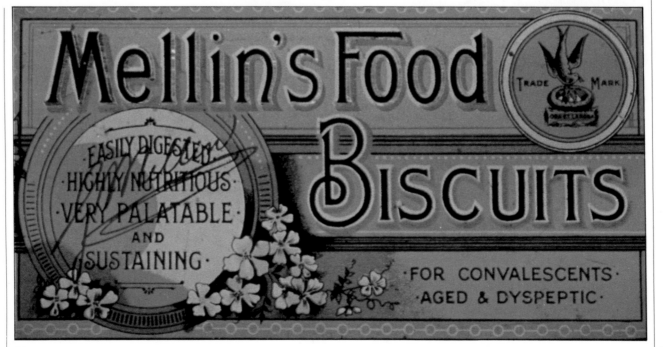

**7**

5 *E.Herbert and Co. French coffee packaging, Britain, c.1915.* **6** *Cherry toothpaste packaging, Britain, c.1880.* **7** *Mellin's Food Biscuit packaging, Britain, c.1900.*

# PACKAGING

1 Bisto Tin, Britain, c.1930.
2 Lifebuoy soap label, Britain, c.1930. 3 Paindor beer label, France, 1925. 4 Anjou wine label, France, c.1920.
5 Camembert cheese label, France, 1914. 6 Montagut poster for stationery store, France, c.1900.

7 Strothmann Schnapps label, Germany, c.1930.
8 Jean Girand fils eau-de-Cologne label, France, 1925. 9 Wisk scouring powder label, Britain, c.1920.

10 Devonshire cider label, Britain, 1920. 11 Vino Flirt, digestive tonic, France, c.1930. 12 Robin starch packet, Britain, c.1930. 13 Liver salts and other packaging, Britain, 1905.

20

WHITEWAY'S DEVONSHIRE Guaranteed pure CYDER.

REG. Nº 26974

9

10

GRAN APERITIVO
VINO FLIRT
EXQUISITO
ESTOMACAL
TONICO
DIGESTIVO
"FLIRT" DA FUERZA
EL FLIRT DA FUERZA
BILBAO

11

REGISTERED TRADE MARK
ROBIN
The New Starch
For Hot & Cold Water Starching.

12

WISK CLEANS TIN LIKE SILVER BRASS LIKE GOLD

IT SCOURS
BUT DOES NOT SCRATCH
REMOVES GREASE LIKE
GREASED LIGHTNING ~
SAVES ELBOW GREASE,
IS FINELY GROUND,
& NOT ONLY REMOVES STAINS,
BUT CLEANS AND POLISHES.

One of the famous "NEW-PIN" Preparations.

13

MARIENBAD
LIVER SALTS

CASHMERE BOUQUET TALC POWDER

ROYAL SHAMROCK

# PACKAGING

**1** *1910.*

**2** *1888-1960.*

**3** *1925-30.*

**4** *1920.*

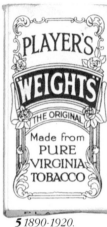

**5** *1890-1920.*

**6** *1930.*

**7** *1930.*

**8** *1920.*

**9** *1920.*

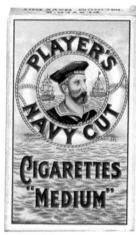

**10** *1920.*

**11** *1910.*

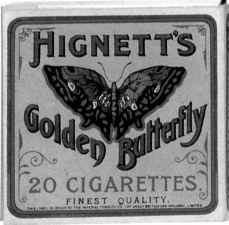

**12** *1900.*

**13** *Late 1920.*

**14** *Late 1920s.*

**15** *1925-30.*

**16** *1900- 1930.*

**17** *Circa 1920s.*

**18** *Late 1920.*

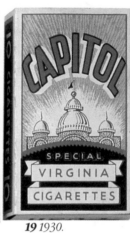

**19** *1930.*

**20** *Late 1920s- 30s.*

**21** *Pre 1930s.*

**22** *1920s.*

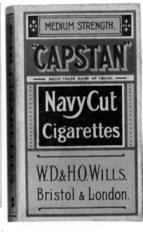

**23** *1920s.*

**24** *1920s.*

**25** *1920s.*

**1900-30.*

**27** *1920s.*

**28** *1900-1930.*

# ADVERTISEMENTS

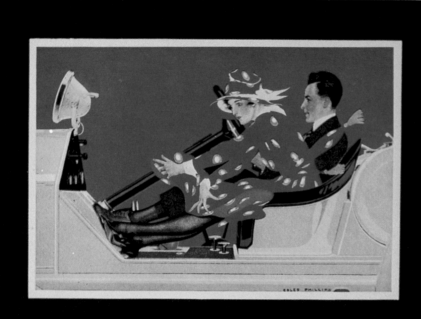

## Luxite Hosiery

LUXITE HOSIERY leaves nothing to be desired in either durability or style. This hosiery has an air about it that is charming and refreshing. It seems to say of those who wear it—"This man knows clothes." Or, "Here is a woman of exquisite taste."

These hose improve with acquaintance, not only because they are shapely and resplendent, but because they retain their beauty regardless of how much they are laundered. Luxite Hosiery is alway pure dyed.

Men's and women's styles are made of pure Japanese silk—many strands to the thread. Also of fine lisle, mercerized cotton and Gold-Ray (scientific silk) for men, women and children.

*The principal stores can supply you. The few who do not have these hose in stock can get them for you if you insist—and you should. For once you know Luxite you won't be content with ordinary hosiery.*

**LUXITE TEXTILES, Inc.,** 636 Fowler Street, Milwaukee, Wisconsin
*Makers of High Grade Hosiery Since 1875*

NEW YORK          CHICAGO          SAN FRANCISCO          LIVERPOOL

### It Puts Off Old Age

by nourishing the entire system.
Quaker Oats makes your blood tingle; nerves strong and steady; brain clear and active; muscles powerful. It makes flesh rather than fat, but enough fat for reserve force.
It builds children up symmetrically into brainy and robust men and women.

You can work on **Quaker Oats** It stays by you.

*At all grocers in 2 lb. Packages only.*

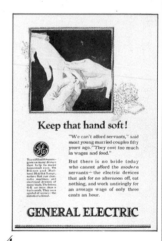

### Keep that hand soft!

"We can't afford servants," said most young married couples fifty years ago. "They cost too much in wages and food."

But there is no bride today who cannot afford the modern servants—the electric devices that ask for no afternoon off, eat nothing, and work untiringly for an average wage of only three cents an hour.

**GENERAL ELECTRIC**

*1 Luxite Hosiery advertisements, Coles Phillips, US, 1918. 2 Bosch Licht advertisement, Lucian Bernhard, Germany, c.1920s.*

*3 Quaker Oats cereal advertisement, US, 1902. 4 General Electric advertisement, US, 1923.*

**5** *GUM department store advertisement 'GUM has the best carpets' and 'Comfort does not cost a lot — moderately cheap and can be paid for in instalments', text Vladimir Mayakovsky, design Alexander Rodchenko, USSR, 1923.*
**6** *Camel cigarettes advertisement, US, 1920.*
**7** *Victrola advertisement, with 'His Master's Voice' trademark, US, 1922.*

# POSTERS

**1**

**2**

**3**

**4**

1 *Automobile exhibition poster, Lucian Bernhard, Germany, 1911.* **2** *Manoli cigarettes, Lucian Bernhard, Germany, 1911.* **3** *Broyhan beer, Paul Scheurich, Germany, 1911.* **4** *Ver Sacrum, Koloman Moser, Germany, 1902.* **5** *'Le Bal Negre', theatre poster, Paul Colin, France, 1927.* **6** *Blanc poster, France, 1920.* **7** *'Zog cleans white paint', poster, Britain, c.1910.* **8** *Ludendorff Fund for the War Wounded, Ludwig Hohlwein, Germany, 1917-18.* **9** *Valentine paint poster, Charles Loupot, France, 1929.* **10** *'The Woman without a Name', film poster, Jan Tschichold, Germany, 1927.*

5

6

8

7

**11** *'The Cabinet of Dr Caligari',
film poster, Marcel Vertes, 1920.*

9

10

11

1 *Cunard Line Europe America, 1925.* 2 *'This is the way to Peace', Lucian Bernhard, Germany, 1917-18.* 3 *Cunard Line Europe America, 1925.*

4 'A Gaiety Girl', theatre poster, Dudley Hardy, Britain, c.1894. 5 Pears' soap, Alf Cooke, Britain, c.1890. 6 'U-Boats Out!', Hans Rudi Erdt, Germany, 1919. 7 'I Want You For US Army', James Montgomery Flagg, US, 1917. 8 'Britons — (Lord Kitchener) Wants You', Alfred Leete, Britain, 1915. 9 'Endurance, Strength and Energy', advertisement for candy, Ludwig Hohlwein, Germany, 1917-1918.

# MAGAZINES

1

2

1 Four covers from the 'Filmkunst' series, Piet Zwart, Holland, c.1928. 2 Cover and poster for Simplicissimus magazine, Thomas Theodor Heine, Germany, 1897. 3 Mer. magazine (Anna Blume), Kur. Schwitters, Germany, 1922.

3

**4** *Theatre and Music No 35, Georgi Stenberg, Moscow, October 1923.* **5** *Modes et Travaux magazine, Paris, 1928.* **6** *Vogue magazine (millinery issue), London, 1914.* **7** *'Epopeya' literary journal, cover by El Lissitizky, Moscow, 1922.*

# JOURNALS

# BOOKS

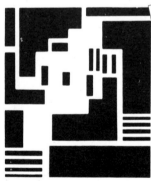

MAANDBLAD GEWIJD AAN
DE MODERNE BEELDENDE
VAKKEN EN KULTUUR
RED. THEO VAN DOESBURG.
**2**

**5**

**1** Notice of an 'Atheistic Easter Festival' from 'The Mind and Face of Bolshevism', USSR, published London 1927. **2** The journal 'De Stijl', cover by Vilmos Huszar, Holland, 1917. **3** The periodical 'Der Dada', cover by Raoul Hausmann, Germany, 1919. **4** Programme cover, Stanley Morison, Britain, 1928. **5** The Prologue, Chaucer's Canterbury Tales, William Morris and the Kelmscott Press, Britain, 1890s. **6** Mayakovsky's 'For the Voice', El Lissitzky, Germany, 1923. **7** One of a series of 17 montages by Yuri Rozhkov

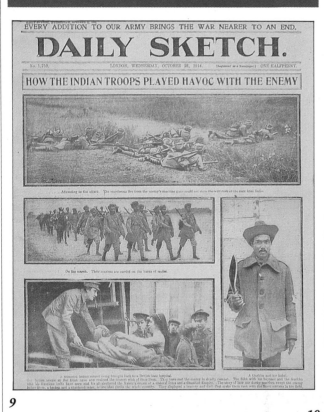

6

7

8

illustrating Mayakovsky's poem 'To the Workers of Kursk', USSR, 1924. **8** 'How to Drive a Motorcar', written and illustrated by the staff of 'The Motor', Britain, 1914. **9** The Daily Sketch newspaper, Britain, 1914. **10** The Daily Mirror newspaper, Britain, 1914.

9

10

# SYMBOLS AND TRADEMARKS

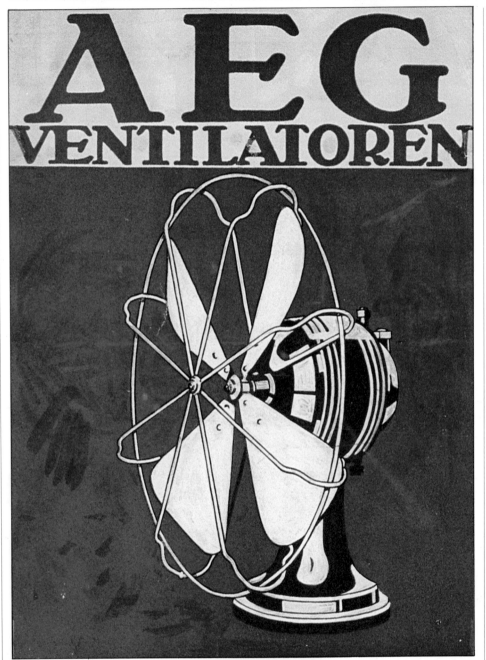

1

You know it by this.

"HIS MASTER'S VOICE."

2

3

4

5

Germany, c.1907. *5 Statliche Bauhaus symbol, from a design by Oskar Schlemmer, Germany, 1922. 6 Personal logo, Piet Zwart, Holland, c.1927.*
*7 Trade symbols from Klingspor Type Foundry catalogue, F.H.Ehmoke and others, Germany, c.1907.*

7

6

*1 Artwork showing AEG logo, Peter Behrens, Germany, c.1908. 2 HMV Records trademark, US, adopted 1901. 3 Type composition (Reklama Mechano), Henryk Berlewi, Warsaw, c.1925. 4 Trade symbol (printing), F.H.Ehmoke,*

# TYPOGRAPHY

ABCDEFGHIJKLMNOPQRSTUV
WXYZ 1234567890

abcdefghijklmnopqrstuvwxyz

ABCDEFGHIJKLMN
OPQRSTUVWXYZ
1234567890

ABCDEFG HIJKLMNO PQR ſ S ſſ
TUVWXYZ&!?
abcdefghijklmno pqrſstuvw
x yz
1234567890

ABCDEFGHIJKLMNOPQ
Rſ S SS ſſ STUVWXYZ&!?
1234567890

1 *Hobo, Morris F. Benton, American Typefounders, US, 1910.*

2 *Neuland, Rudolf Koch, Klingspor, Germany, 1923.*

3 *Broadway, M.F.Benton, American Typefounders, US, 1929.*

4 *Broadway Inline, M.F.Benton, Lanston Monotype, US, 1928-29.*

# TYPOGRAPHY

ABCDEFGHIJKLMNOPQRST
UVWXYZ&?!

**1** Copperplate Gothic, Frederic Goudy, American Typefounders, US, 1901.

ABCDEFGHIJKLMNOPQRS
TUVWXYZ&?!

**2** Copperplate Gothic Heavy, Frederick Goudy, American Typefounders, US, 1901.

ABCDEFGHIJKLMNOPQRSTUVWXY
abcdefghijklmnopqrſstuvwxyz
1234567890

ABCDEFGHIJKLMNOPQRSTUVWXY
abcdefghijklmnopqrſstuvwxyz

**3** Belwe Roman, Georg Belwe, Schelter & Giesecke, 1926.

ABCDEFGHIJKLMNOPQRSTUV
WXYZ
abcdefghijklmnopqrsſtuvwxyz
1234567890

**4** Eckmann, Otto Eckmann, Klingspor, Germany, 1900.

ABCDEFGHIJKLMNOPQRSTUVWXY
abcdefghijklmnopqrstuvwxyz
£1234567890$

**5** Copper Black, Oswald Cooper, American Typefounders for Barnhart & Spindler, US, 1921.

ABCDEFGHIJKLMNOPQRSTUVWXYZ
abcdefghijklmnopqrstuvwxyz
1234567890

**6** *Corvinnus, Imre Reiner, Bauer, Germany, 1929-34.*

ABCDEFGHIJKLMNOPQRSTUVWXYZ
abcdefghijklmnopqrstuvwxyz
1234567890

**7** *Bembo, copy of a roman cut by Francesco Griffo for Aldus Manutius in the 15th century, Monotype, 1929.*

ABCDEFGHIJKLMNOPQRSTUVWXYZ
abcdefghijklmnopqrstuvwxyz
1234567890

**8** *Franklin Gothic Extra Condensed, M.F.Benton, American Typefounders, US, 1903-12.*

ABCDEFGHIJKLMNOPQRSTUVWXYZ
abcdefghijklmnopqrstuvwxyz
1234567890

**9** *Franklin Gothic Condensed, M.F.Benton, American Typefounders, US, 1903-12.*

ABCDEFGHIJKLMNOPQRSTUVWXYZ
abcdefghijklmnopqrstuvwxyz
1234567890

**10** *News Gothic, M.F.Benton, American Typefounders, US, 1908.*

# TYPOGRAPHY

ABCDEFGHIJKLMNOP
QRSTUVWXYZ
abcdefghijklmnopqrst
uvwxyz
1234567890 & £

ABCDEFGHIJKLMNOPQRSTUVWXYZ
abcdefghijklmnopqrstuvwxyz
1234567890

ABCDEFGHIJKLMNOPQRSTUVWXYZ
123456789o

ABCDEFGHIJKLMNOPQRSTUVWXYZ
abcdefghijklmnopqrstuvwxyz
1234567890

ABCDEFGHIJKLMNOPQRSTUVWXYZ
abcdefghijklmnopqrstuvwxyz
1234567890

ABCDEFGHIJKLMNOPQRSTUVWXYZ

abcdefghijklmnopqrstuvwxyz

1234567890

**6** *Futura Light, Paul Renner, Bauer, Germany, 1927-30,*

ABCDEFGHIJKLMNOPQRSTUVWXYZ

abcdefghijklmnopqrstuvwxyz

1234567890

**7** *Futura Light Condensed, Paul Renner, Bauer, Germany, 1927-30.*

**ABCDEFGHIJKLMNOPQRSTUV WXYZ abcdefghijklmnopqrstuvwxyz 1234567890**

**8** *Futura Bold, Paul Renner, Bauer, Germany, 1927-30.*

# BANK NOTES

**1** *Banco de Espana, 500 pesetas, Spain, c.1920.* **2** *Silk bank note, Bielefeld Berlin, Germany, 1922.* **3** *100 mark note, Reichsbank, Germany, 1920.*

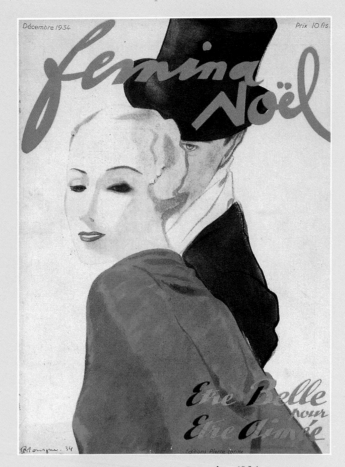

*Femina Noel, France, December, 1934.*

# CHAPTER · TWO

# 1930
## TO
# 1939

# INTRODUCTION

The 1929 financial crash on Wall Street moved a tidal wave of economic disaster around the industrialized world. Nowhere was this more felt than in Germany, where the number of unemployed rose from two million in 1929 to six million in 1932. Three years later in 1932, Franklin Delano Roosevelt was elected President of the United States. Roosevelt's 'New Deal' policy used federal works as a measure to reduce unemployment. Highway construction and the famous Tennessee Valley Authority (TVA) project were all part of this massive work creation scheme.

Britain also used public works to alleviate unemployment. After 1933 an unprecedented house building boom played a major role in providing jobs. London continued to be the largest city in the world as housing estates, arterial roads and factories pushed outwards into the countryside. New industries provided the middle classes with mass-produced family cars and modern household electrical goods. Many of the companies in this sector of manufacturing were American owned and advertising adopted 'scientific' methods to promote an expanding home market. Britain's rearmament programme, which started in 1936, also gave impetus to financial recovery. However, a working-class generation would remember for decades the marches of the unemployed to London during the depression years.

In November 1936 the BBC inaugurated the world's first public television service. Radar was another electronic innovation under development in Britain at this time. Along with the Supermarine Spitfire (developed from experience gained with the Schneider Trophy winning seaplanes of the early 1930s), it would play a decisive role in the 1940 Battle of Britain.

### Britain

At the end of the nineteenth century 'advertisers' agents' already existed in London, but the growth of modern advertising agencies did not take place until after the First World War. The 1930s saw the slow decline of the publicity studios attached to printing houses. In 1930 the progressive advertising agencies were typified by Highams, W.S. Crawford, S.H. Benson and Stuarts Advertising. It was a period when the publicity policies of great corporations were decided more often that not by one man. Giants of the new twentieth century corporate world being Frank Pick of the Underground Group, Jack Beddington of Shell-Mex BP Limited and Sir Stephen Tallents of the General Post Office.

The increased use of motor vehicles and the progress of civil aviation meant assured business for the big oil companies. The publicity strategy of Shell was formulated by Jack Beddington (1893-1959), who joined the company in 1927. As at London Transport, Shell used the finest names in the British art world. Press advertising caught the attention of the public with witty copywriting and the use of artists like Edward Bawden, Rex Whistler, H.M. Bateman and Nicolas Bentley.

The BBC and the national airline, Imperial Airways, both represented new organisations which came into existence through technological progress after the First World War. Again they followed the lead shown by the Underground as public patrons of good art and design. The BBC published the *Radio Times*, *The Listener* and a series of radio talks booklets. A notable feature of BBC publications was the wood engraved work of Eric Ravilious (1903-1942). Imperial Airways commissioned abstract painted designs for posters from Ben Nicholson (1889-1982) and Theyre Lee-Elliot; the latter having created the world famous 'Speed-bird' mark in 1932.

A typographic renaissance was also taking place. Unlike the private press movement before 1914, modern mechanical type composition was used and the need to improve the appearance of popular printed matter recognized. In 1932 Stanley Morison designed his famous 'Times New Roman' typeface for *The Times* newspaper. His 'yellow' dust jackets for Victor Gollancz's books gave them an almost Dadaist look. Penguin Books, founded in 1935 by Allen Lane (1903-1970), brought high design standards to inexpensive paperback books. In the production department at Penguin's was 22-year-old Edward Young, who created the earliest version of the Penguin publishing device and arranged the typographic style of the covers. These had

**WINTER SALES** are best reached by **UNDERGROUND**

Frank Pick (1878-1941) joined the Underground in 1906. By 1928 he had risen to become its Joint Managing Director. Under Pick's guidance the house style of the Underground, together with the London General Omnibus Company which it owned, acquired a unique place in the history of applied design. Along with Peter Behren's AEG work, it was a very early example of what later would be known as corporate identity. Notable graphic elements were the 'Underground' or 'Railway' letterform initially devised by Edward Johnston in 1916 the distinctive 'bull's eye' symbol, also largely the work of Johnston after the First World War (an archaic form existed in 1905)

and most important publicity posters. In 1933 the Underground Group was absorbed by a newly created public corporation, London Transport. Pick then became its Vice-Chairman.

Pick's prominence in the London Transport structure has tended to eclipse the role of Christian Barman (1889-1980). Barman, who was invited by Pick to become Publicity officer of London Transport in 1935, continued and expanded its design reputation. From 1915 Pick had used American-born E. McKnight Kauffer (1890-1954) to design posters for the Underground Group and during the 1920s graphic work by many famous artists had graced tube station walls.

different weights of 'Monotype' Gill Sans for emphasis. The books themselves were mechanically composed on 'Monotype' equipment.

The period between the wars was when 'Monotype' letterpress equipment and typefaces reached their definitive stage. Typographic consultants to the Monotype Corporation were Stanley Morison (1889-1967) and Beatrice Warde (1900-1969). Born Beatrice Becker in New York City, she studied at Columbia University and married Frederick Warde, Printer to Princeton University. Beatrice Warde was Assistant Librarian at American Type Founders (ATF) between 1921-25. In 1925 she travelled to Paris where she made extensive studies into the history of French typefaces. In Britain she became editor of the *Monotype Recorder* in 1927, and in addition wrote typographic articles under the pseudonym 'Paul Beaujon'.

One of the journals which Paul Beaujon and Stanley Morison contributed to was *The Fleuron*, appearing between 1923 and 1930. In November 1935 Oliver Simon of the Curwen Press commenced publication of *Signature*, and again issues featured articles by Beaujon and Morison together with names such as Harry Carter, Holbrook Jackson, Paul Nash and John Piper. The last of the typographic periodicals to appear in the 1930s was *Typography*, founded by Robert Harling, James Shand and Ellic Howe in 1936. Jan Tschichold's article *Type Mixtures* was printed in *Typography No.3* (1937). Other contributions by Tschichold to British typography were the short section he wrote in the book *Circle* (1937) and his work for the printers and publishers Lund Humphries in 1938. This included a redesign of the *Penrose Annual*, under the editorship of R.B. Fishenden.

### France

The end of the 1920s was the great divide as far as modern graphic design was concerned. Typography, often used with photography, would come into its own in Germany and Switzerland. In France drawn pictorial imagery would flourish. Progressive British and American designers, who were working in emergent corporate environments, would draw heavily on German typographic style on the one hand and French art movement treatments on the other. French graphic art during the late 1920s and 1930s would raise poster design to its ultimate form – a model which would be admired internationally for the next two decades.

Jean Carlu abandoned his architectural studies when he lost his right arm as a result of an accident. He was eighteen years of age and started to design posters. Early influences were the French graphic artist Leonetto Cappiello (1875-1942) and the 'synthetic' Cubism of the painters Juan Gris (1887-1927) and Albert Gleizes (1881-1951). In 1932 Carlu became concerned about the issue of disarmament and founded the Office de Propaganda pour la Paix (The Office

A. M. Cassandre (1901-1968), Paul Colin and Jean Carlu were the acknowledged masters of the French poster genre. A unity between lettering and imagery was always a strong feature of Cassandre's posters. In 1925 he made the aquaintance of Charles Peignot, and this resulted in a number of well-known Cassandre typefaces being issued by Deberny & Peignot after 1929. Cassandre worked for overseas clients, among these were posters designed for the London Midland and Scottish Railway (1928), the Dutch advertising agency Nijgh & Van Ditmar (1928-29), and a campaign for Ford V8 car models in the United States (1937). His most famous design was 'Dubo ...Dubon...Dubonnet' (1934).

The Second World War drew an end to this great period of French graphic art. In 1939 Cassandre returned from America in order to serve his country, but like E. McKnight Kauffer his most innovative days were past. Carlu would design a number of fine war posters, including *Journée Franco-Britannique* (1939). Colin's 1940 poster *Silence, l'ennemie guete vos confidences* was issued just before the German offensive of May 1940.

for Graphic Propaganda in the Cause of Peace) in Paris. He handled the advertising for the 1937 Paris Exhibition and in 1939 he went to America in order to organize the *France at War* display at the New York World Fair.

### Switzerland

The 1930s saw Switzerland rise to the forefront of graphic design. Photography would be a major ingredient in transforming Swiss printed matter away from traditional painted and drawn imagery. The work of German 'Neue Sachlichkeit' (new objectivity) photographers became known at the end of the 1920s. The possibilities of photography were also made known by the exhibition 'Die neue Photographie' ('The New Photography'), which took place in Basle in 1931. Basle and Zurich became the natural centres for Swiss graphic design, and as they were the two largest cities in the Confederation major industrial concerns were based on their environs. Swiss art education was founded on vocational requirements and the *Kunstgewerbeschulen* in Basle and Zurich existed to meet these commercial demands. The closing event of the decade in Switzerland was the 1939 Landesausstellung (LA, National Exhibition) in Zurich. Both Hans Neuburg (1904-1983) and Müller-Brockmann carried out exhibition design in various pavilions.

The origins of modern Swiss graphic design can be traced back to Max Bill, Anton Stankowski and Jan Tschichold. Bill studied first at the Kunstgewerbeschule (School of Art and Crafts) in Zurich and then at the Bauhaus, 1927-29. He was, and is, the true embodiment of the 'Renaissance man' concept in that he was an architect, painter, sculptor, industrial designer and art theorist. A

# INTRODUCTION

number of Swiss pioneers formed a 'Zurich Group' around Max Bill. These were Camille Graeser, Richard Paul Lohse, Hans Neuburg and Josef Müller-Brockmann.

In 1933 Tschichold was forced to leave Germany. His books, in particular *Die neue Typographie* (*The New Typography*), published in 1928, had made an impression in Switzerland. In 1935 *Typographische Gestaltung* (*Typographic Design*) appeared, which Tschichold wrote while he worked for the Basle publishing house Benno Schwabe & Co.

Other important Zurich designers were Otto Baumberger (1889-1961), Herbert Matter (1907-1984) and Emil Schulthess. Both Matter and Schulthess combined photographic imagery and type in a similar manner. In 1936 Matter emigrated to the United States. Schulthess became art editor of the magazine *Du* in 1941. Since 1957 he has freelanced as a photographer.

## Germany

On 30 January 1933 Adolf Hitler was appointed German Chancellor, and the Nazis quickly sought to remove their political rivals. The Bauhaus moved to an empty telephone factory in the Steglitz district of Berlin. On 20 July 1933 the Nazis compelled Mies van der Rohe to dissolve the Bauhaus. Manifestations inspired by the modern movement, including non-serifed typefaces, were denounced as 'cultural Bolshevism'. Art styles derived from Cubism were also derided as 'degenerate art'. Exhibitions of *Entartete Kunst* ('degenerate art') comprising confiscated works of art were staged in Hamburg and Munich. Vierthaler's 1936 poster parodies El Lissitsky's *With the red wedge hit the whites!* and mocks with its use of Paul Renner's Futura typeface. An outpouring of racial propaganda now began to castigate Jews and steps were taken to ban negro entertainment forms such as jazz.

Not only were fine artists forced to leave Germany. Hans Schleger ('Zéró') was a German Army veteran of the First World War. He made his name as a graphic designer in the United States during the 1920s before returning to Berlin, where he worked for the German office of W.S. Crawford. Schleger left for Britain in 1933. Berthold Wolpe had studied under Rudolf Koch in Offenbach and designed his Hyperion typeface for Bauer in 1932. Wolpe decided to leave in 1935. Hans Unger studied with Jupp Wiertz (1888-1939). In 1936 he emigrated to South Africa.

Under Goebbels, State Minister for Propaganda and People's Enlightenment, film, broadcasting and the printed media were co-ordinated to promote the idea of a new 'Greater Germany'. A focus to this was the figure of Adolf Hitler. After Hindenburg's death, he became the 'Führer' of the German Reich. Typical of the inscriptions raising Hitler to deity status were 'Wer ein Volk retten will, kann nur heroisch denken' ('the man who has saved a people, can only think heroically') and 'Ein Volk, ein Reich, ein Führer'

*Pastificio Triestino pasta advertisement, Italy, 1931.*

*Dole Pineapple Co., fruit juice advertisement, A.M. Cassandre, US/France, c.1939.*

**1** *German Airways advertisement, Otto Arpke, Germany, c.1930.*

('One people, one state, one leader'). The national identity 'problem' of the German flag – the Nazis disliked the socialist connotation of the black, red and yellow horizontal tricolour – was 'solved' by the adoption of the swastika flag.

## Italy

Although Benito Mussolini had established a Fascist dictatorship in Italy on 28 October 1922, much commercial advertising during the 1930s made little if any reference to the 'New Roman Empire'. Indeed, the Italian members of the avant-garde followed the liberal traditions of the European graphic design profession.

In 1933 the Studio Boggeri was founded in Milan by Antonio Boggeri. Xanti Schawinsky was a Bauhaus trained designer who worked for the studio. Two famous names in European type design, Paul Renner (1878-1956) and Imre Reiner, were both associated with the Studio Boggeri.

Other Italian designers of note were Severo Pozzatti ('Sepo') and Marcello Dudovich (1878-1962). However, Fascist posters in comparison to the mainstream of Italian graphic design were generally weak and lacked the power shown by Mussolini's architectural edifices.

## The United States

In 1933 the painter George Biddle, a friend of Roosevelt, wrote to the President suggesting the employment of artists by the government on Federal jobs. He pointed out that in Mexico artists were being successfully used on mural schemes and received a wage for their labours. As a result, the Public Works of Art Project came into being. Although this was short-lived it served as a pilot scheme for the Federal Art Project, which was run by the WPA between 1935 and 1939. Many previously unemployed painters turned their skills to poster design.

Roosevelt's 'New Deal' achieved the miracle of economic recovery and American design became characterized by the streamline industrial designs of Norman Bel Geddes and Raymond Loewy. In 1934 Chrysler marketed their 'Airflow' model. After 1936 the advertising copy for cars and oil products conveyed a feeling that economic matters had returned to normal.

The situation in Germany had forced many graphic designers to seek new careers in the United States. Moholy-Nagy arrived in Chicago to head the 'New Bauhaus'. Herbert Bayer (1900-1985) set about work in New York with exhibition design for the *Bauhaus* 1919-1928 held at the Museum of Modern Art in 1938.

In 1939 Roosevelt's unique social experiment came to an end and even the New York World's Fair could not escape the reality that the world was on the verge of war. The strap line to Joseph Binder's World Fair poster proclaimed 'The World of Tomorrow' – a world which unknown to its visitors would shortly bring the atomic bomb.

THE AMAZING
OXYGEN WASHER

**Persil**

REGISTERED

Makes the linens *clean*
and therefore
perfectly white
also best for silks and woollens

JOSEPH CROSFIELD & SONS LTD. WARRINGTON.

1

CHOCOLAT GARANTI PUR CACAO ET SUCRE

CONFISERIE REGIS PATISSERIE

CHOCOLAT **Regis**

TABLETTE DE 250 GRS

2

THESE CRYSTALS CONTAIN NO MILK

MILK

**CRYSTELLA**

JELLY

CRYSTALS

3

1 *Pack for Persil, washing flakes, Britain, c.1930.* 2 *Regis chocolate bar wrapper, France, c.1932.* 3 *Crystella milk jelly crystals pack, Milner Gray, Britain, c.1939.* 4 *Gold Flake* cigarettes, point of sale display card, Britain, c.1935. 5 *OK Sauce label, Britain, c.1930.* 6 *British soft drinks labels, c.1938.*

MASON'S
DELICIOUS

'O.K'
SAUCE
REGISTERED

PIQUANT
AND
APPETISING

OF Guaranteed
Purity and
Digestive Merit

EXCELS WITH CHOPS,
STEAKS, VEAL CUTLETS,
COLD MEATS, FISH &c &c

MADE IN ENGLAND BY
GEORGE MASON & Cº
LIMITED

CHELSEA WORKS
LONDON
ENGLAND

5

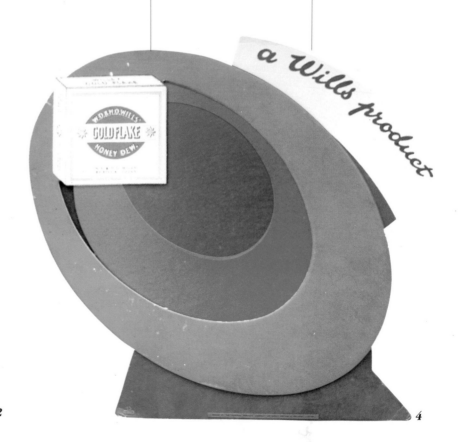

a Wills product

W.D.&H.O.WILLS
GOLD FLAKE
HONEY DEW

4

Quality
CHERRY CIDERETTE

X.1

Quality
DELIGHTFUL
CIDERETTE

X.2

AMERICAN
CREAM
SODA

X.3

COOL & REFRESHING
ICE CREAM
SODA

X.4

SUPERIOR QUALITY
Aromatic
GINGER
ALE
WHOLESOME
DELICIOUS

X.7

Old Fashioned
Ginger Beer
Quality

X.8

Old
Fashioned
Stone
Ginger Beer

X.9

GRAPE FRUIT
PERFECT
FLAVOUR

X.10

LEMON
BARLEY
Refreshing

X.13

LEMON
CRUSH
Quality

X.14

Quality
LEMON SQUASH

X.15

LIME JUICE & SODA
BEST OF ALL AND
MOST DELICIOUS

X.16

ORANGE
CHAMPAGNE

X.19

ORANGE CRUSH
QUALITY
AND
FLAVOUR

X.20

ORANGE JUICE
QUALITY
AND
FLAVOUR

X.21

Pineapple
DELICIOUS

X.22

1 *Camembert cheese box label, France, c.1930.* 2 *Sanatogen bottle label, Britain, c.1930.* 3 *Shredded Wheat packet,* Britain, c. 1938. 4 *Berlat chocolate bar wrapper, France, c.1932.*

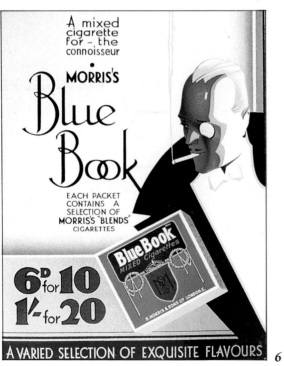

5 *Fry's 5 Centre chocolates, point of sale display card, Britain, c.1932.* 6 *Blue Book cigarettes, point of sale display card, Britain, c.1935.* 7 *Tolima chocolate bar wrapper, France, c.1932.* 8 *State Express 333 cigarettes, point of sale display card, Britain, c.1930.*

# ADVERTISEMENTS

**Pity the poor fish that never has a Guinness**

GUINNESS FOR STRENGTH

**5**

*1 Tri-ang pedal cars, magazine advertisement, Britain, c.1935. 2 The Lincoln car, US, c.1930. 3 Humber motor cars, Britain, c.1930. 4 Hillman cars, magazine advertisement, Britain, c.1930. 5 Guinness, magazine advertisement, Benson advertising agency, Britain, c.1935. 6 Chesterfield cigarettes, advertisement, US, 1931.*

# GOOD .. they've got to be good!

THEY'RE MILDER, FRED

TASTE BETTER, TOO!

*Fred and Adele Astaire in Broadway's musical hit, "The Band Wagon"*

## Darn good — you'll say!

Everybody wants a mild cigarette. And when you find one that is milder and *tastes better* too—you've got a smoke! Chesterfields are so much milder that you can smoke as many as you like. Mild, ripe, sweet-tasting tobaccos — the best that money can buy. That's what it takes to make a cigarette as good as Chesterfield. And the *purest* cigarette paper!

Every Chesterfield is well-filled. Burns evenly. Smokes cool and comfortable. *They Satisfy* sums it all up!

**EVERYBODY'S GETTING ON "THE BAND WAGON"**

*Chesterfield*

CIGARETTES

LIGGETT & MYERS TOBACCO CO.

**6**

51

EVERYWHERE YO

THE RYE MARSHES

YOU CAN BE SURE C

J GO

PAUL NASH

SHELL

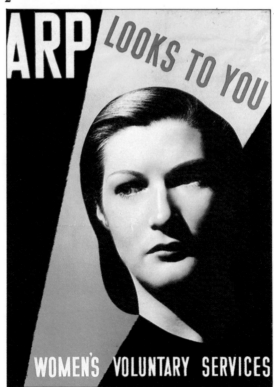

1 *Shell, lorry bill, Paul Nash,*
*Britain, 1932.* 2 *Bellagio*
*Grand Hotel, Italy, c.1930.*
3 *Air Raid Precautions poster,*
*Britain, 1938.* 4 *Mossant hats,*
*Leonetto Cappiello, France,*
*1938.*

# POSTERS

1 *Poster on agricultural modernisation and reform, Gustav Klutsis, USSR, 1931.*
2 *'Normandie' advertisement, A.M.Cassandre, France, 1935.*
3 *Advertisement for British Airways Ltd, Theyre Lee-Elliot, Britain, c.1939.* 4 *Exhibition poster, Jean Carlu, France, 1937.* 5 *Railway poster, Charles Loupot, France, 1930.*
6 *Aid for Spain, poster, Joan Miró, Spain, c.1937.* 7 *English language propaganda poster, Spain, c.1937.*

4

5

7

# MAGAZINES AND JOURNALS

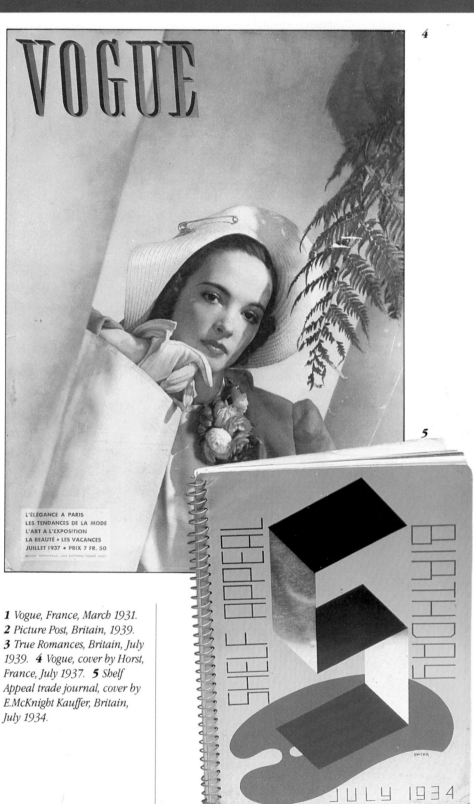

1 *Vogue, France, March 1931.*
2 *Picture Post, Britain, 1939.*
3 *True Romances, Britain, July 1939.* 4 *Vogue, cover by Horst, France, July 1937.* 5 *Shelf Appeal trade journal, cover by E.McKnight Kauffer, Britain, July 1934.*

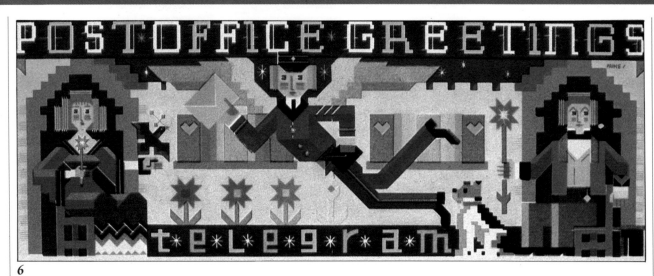

6

6 Post Office telegram, Britain, c.1938.
7 Arabia tea, coffee and cocoa products leaflet, Austria, 1938.
8 Air Union English language information, France, c.1935.

7

# AIR UNION

# AIR UNION

## FREIGHT SERVICE

## TRAVEL BY AIR

THE FASTEST GOODS EXPRESS TO THIRTY EUROPEAN CITIES

PLEASURE COMFORT SPEED REGULARITY SAFETY

DEVAMBEZ

8

# BOOKS

ARIEL

ANDRÉ MAUROIS

THE BODLEY HEAD

PENGUIN BOOKS

A PELICAN SPECIAL

ANTHONY BERTRAM

DESIGN

1931

ВЛАДИМИР МАЯКОВСКИЙ

*La Bella Scrittura*

NELLE SCUOLE ELEMENTARI

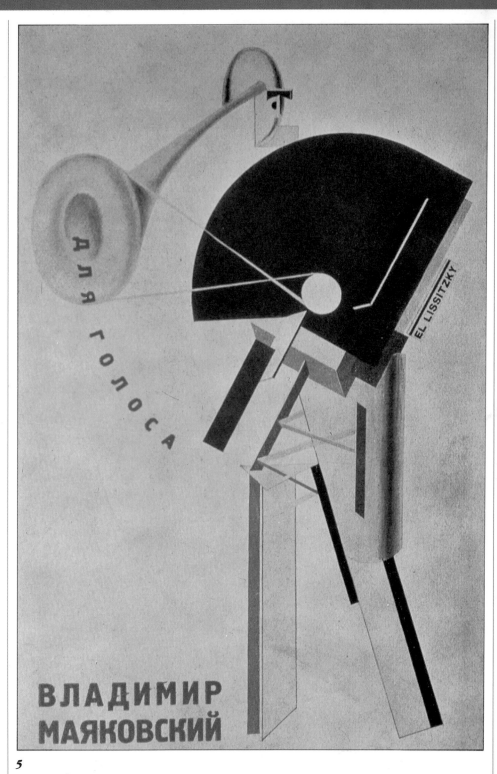

ВЛАДИМИР МАЯКОВСКИЙ

**1** *Jacket for 'Ariel' by André Maurois, the first Penguin, Britain, July 1935.* **2** *Pelican Special Design by Anthony Bertram, Britain, December 1938.* **3** *'Elephants in the Komsomol' by Mayakovsky, cover by El Lissitsky, USSR, 1931.* **4** *'La Bella Scrittura' cover, Verlag fur Schriftkunde Heintze and Blanckertz, Germany, c.1938.* **5** *Title page 'For The Voice', El Lissitsky, USSR, 1923.*

SYLVIA THOMPSON

"THIRD ACT IN VENICE"

**6** *Jacket for 'Third Act in Venice', C.W.Bacon, Britain, c.1935.* **7** *Chapter heading in 'The Four Gospels', Eric Gill, Britain, 1931.*

AND IT CAME TO PASS IN THOSE DAYS, THAT THERE WENT OUT A DECREE

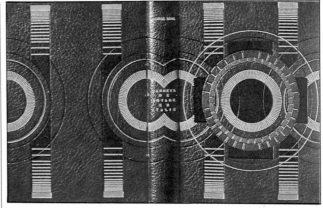

**9**

**8**

**10**

**11**

**8** *Endpapers, 'The Story of 25 Eventful Years in Pictures', Britain, 1935.* **9** *Binding for 'Carnets de Voyage en Italie' by Maurice Oldham, Pierre Le Grain, France, c.1930.* **10** *Title page, 'The Story of 25 Eventful Years in Pictures', Britain, 1935.* **11** *Morocco binding for 'Le Paradis Musulman' by Dr. Mardrus, François-Louis Schmied, France, c.1930.*

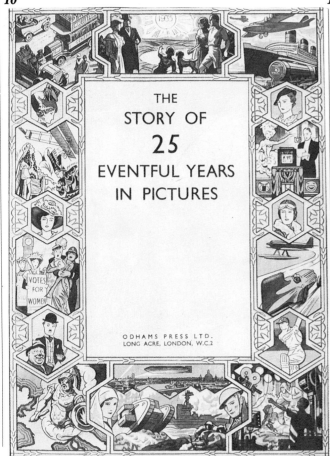

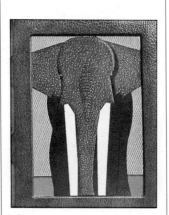

**12**

**12** *Binding for 'Le Livre de la Jungle' by Rudyard Kipling, Louis Creuzevault, France, c.1930.*

# SYMBOLS AND TRADEMARKS

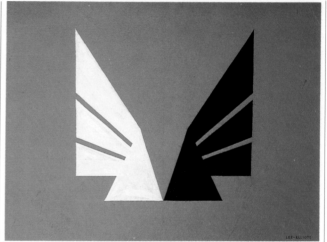

1 *Badge for ARP units, Britain, 1938.* 2 *Air Mail wings, Theyre Lee-Elliot, Britain, c.1936.* 3 *NRA code, US, 1933.*

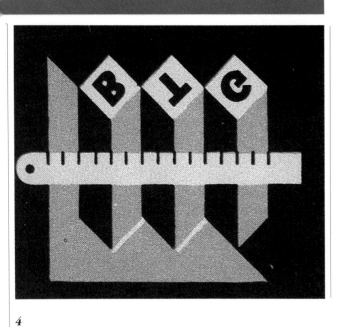

4

5

# INFORMATION DESIGN

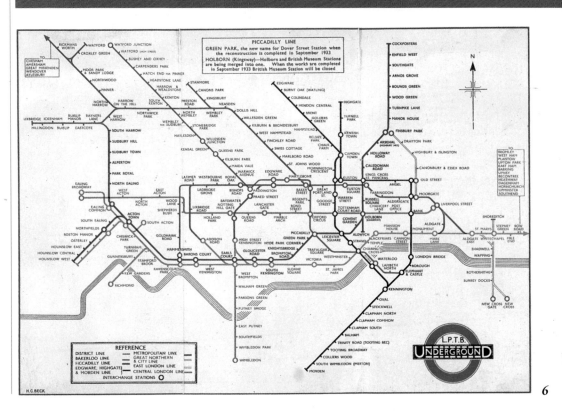

**4** *British Typographers Guild logo, from 1939 membership card, Britain.* **5** *London Transport Bull's Eye symbol, Britain, 1933.* **6** *London Transport Underground network diagram, H.C.Beck, Britain, 1933.*

6

# TYPOGRAPHY

ABCDEFGHIJKLMNOPQRSTUVWXYZ&
abcdefghijklmnopqrstuvwxyz

ABCDEFGHIJKLMNOPQRSTUVWXYZ
abcdefghijklmnopqrstuvwxyz
1234567890

ABCDEFGHIJKLMNOPQRSTUVWXYZ&
abcdefghijklmnopqrstuvwxyz
1234567890

ABDEGHJKMNPQRSTUVWXYZ
1234567890

# FREGIO RAZIONALE

FREGIO RAZIONALE

ABCDEFGHIJKLMNOPQRSTUVXYZW
1234567890

6 Razionale, G.da Milano, Nebiolo, Italy, 1935.

ABCDEFGHIJKLMNOPQRSTUVWXYZ
abcdefghijklmnopqrstuvwxyz
1 2 3 4 5 6 7 8 9 0

7 *Rockwell, Monotype, 1934.*

ABCDEFGHIJKLMNOPQRSTUVWXYZ
abcdefghijklmnopqrstuvwxyz
1234567890

8 *City, Georg Trump, Berthold, 1930.*

Lanson

The

proudest

Champagne

of France

9 *Lettering from advertisement for Lanson Champagne, R.J.Batterbury, Britain, late 1930s.*

Two men of 287,000 ! They make steel. Steel to safeguard our safeguard, the ships of the Navy. Steel which gives swift strength to the Queen Mary, rugged endurance to an icebreaker, and to the tramp steamer the power to plug along for ever. Steel — safest of all — in normal use and in emergency.

Steel has a strength all its own, and scientific shaping will multiply that strength. Steel rolled into girders is stronger than massive bars. Corrugate a steel sheet and you stiffen it tenfold.

THE BRITISH STEELWORK ASSOCIATION, WESTMINSTER, S.W.I.

1

TELEPHONE **LESS**

2

# Simpson
### ICCADILLY

3

**1** British Steelwork Association advertisement, Mather & Crowther, Britain, c.1939. **2** 'Telephone Less' lettering by Hans Schleger, Britain, c.1939. **3** Lettering for advertising material for Simpson, Piccadilly, Ashley Havinden, Britain, c.1935.

# SOUVERAINES

**4** Acier Noir, A.M.Cassandre, Deberny & Peignot, France, 1936.

# DANGER

**5** Bifur, A.M.Cassandre, Deberny & Peignot, France, c.1930.

ABCDEFGHIJKLMNOPQRSTUVWXYZ
abcdefghijklmnopqrstuvwxyz
1234567890 1234567890

**6** Peignot Light, A.M.Cassandre, Deberny & Peignot, France, 1937.

ABCDEFGHIJKLMNOPQRSTUVWXYZ
abcdefghijklmnopqrstuvwxyz
1234567890

**7** Peignot, A.M.Cassandre, Deberny & Peignot, France, 1937.

ABCDEFGHIJKLMNOPQRSTUV
WXYZ
abcdefghijklmnopqrstuvwxyz
1234567890 1234567890

**8** Peignot Bold, A.M.Cassandre, Deberny & Peignot, France, 1937.

# STAMPS

**1, 2, 3 & 4** *King George V Silver Jubilee 1910-1935, stamps of ¹/₂d, 1d, 1¹/₂d and 2¹/₂d, Britain, 1935.* **5** *King George VI, 1¹/₂d stamp, Britain, 1937.*

*The British Commonwealth of Nations Together, issued by the MOI, Britain, c.1941.*

# CHAPTER · THREE

# 1940
## TO
# 1949

# INTRODUCTION

Between the wars, film and radio gradually established themselves as powerful mass communication media. Newsreels of air raids shown during the Spanish Civil War made cinema audiences apprehensive. Alexander Korda's 1936 film, *Things to Come*, visually presented a world laid waste by a future war of attrition. The minds of ordinary people could be effectively moved by film. The actuality of the cinema was a powerful force for conveying propaganda, and this potential was not wasted by the dictators.

Radio was an immediate medium and, when used in conjunction with stirring music, highly dramatic. The wartime broadcasts from Germany of William Joyce (Lord Haw-Haw), and those from Japan of Iva Ikudo Toguri (Tokyo Rose) would become synonymous with the meaning of enemy propaganda. In 1914, newspaper placards and official typographic proclamations had informed about the mobilization of the great European powers for war. In 1939, it would be the radio which prepared the people of Europe for war.

During the dark days of the Second World War the radio oratory of Winston Churchill brought hope to the British people and occupied Europe. In 1946, Churchill's prophetic speech, delivered at Fulton, Missouri in 1946, warned that an iron curtain was now descending over Europe. Two years later, the Soviet road, railway and canal blockade of Berlin created the first major crisis between the Western allies and Russia. The cold war had begun.

The printed word still occupied a major place as a propaganda tool, however, and in addition graphic art assumed a new role as a vehicle for conveying public information and morale-boosting exhortations from national leaders during the war and post-war period.

## Germany

The military lessons of the First World War were not forgotten by the German General Staff. A daring strategy of *Blitzkrieg*, or lightning war, was planned. Highly mobile forces would seize key objectives supported by the Luftwaffe (air force). Denmark and Norway were invaded and, in May 1940, a German Western offensive overran Holland, Belgium and France. All the time, behind the fighting troops, PK (propaganda company) camera teams recorded events. Still photography, sometimes in colour, was also important. The film footage would be carefully edited to form either part of the *Deutsche Wochenschau* (German Weekly Newsreel) or triumphant documentaries such as *Sieg im Westen* (*Victory in the West*). Much photography would find its way into *Signal* magazine, which was published with funds provided by the OKW (High Command of the Armed Forces). The format and layout was based on *Life* magazine. Printed with many pages in full-colour photogravure, editions would be produced in the languages of occupied countries. Even

*Air Corps US Army, Joseph Binder, US, 1941.*

English language copies were circulated. Advertising was a clever part of its image, and advertisements for unobtainable or hard-to-come-by consumerables suggested that all was well throughout the Nazi 'New Europe'.

A noticeable feature of German typography during the early part of the war was the continuing use of traditional black gothic letter typeforms. The two main categories were Schwabacher and its later development, Fraktur, which were collectively known as Deutsche Schrift (German lettering). Its use was everywhere to be seen, from painted inscriptions on the walls of a country inn to the lines of type in the NSDAP (Nazi Party) newspaper, *Völkischer Beobachter* (*People's Observer*). Suddenly, on 3 January 1941, a NSDAP circular signed by Martin Bormann ordered that the use of the black gothic lettering be discontinued as soon as was practicable. The reason given by Bormann was that Jews resident in Germany soon after Gutenberg's time had gained control of book printing and introduced the Schwabacher letterform. This was another example of the way in which the Nazis were able to exploit anti-semitic feeling. In reality, the Schwabacher letter was derived from medieval calligraphy and there were no Jewish-owned presses in Germany during the first centuries of printing with moveable type. The likely motive behind this command was that by 1941 the Nazis considered the black gothic lettering too archaic and backward-looking for propaganda purposes. From this point onwards, Roman typefaces gradually appeared in books and newspapers. Simple block lettering was used on posters when Roman forms proved too weak for display use.

## Britain

During the Second World War, recruiting posters were only required for home defence, volunteer branches of the services and the women's auxiliary forces until the National Service Act was rushed through parliament on 2 September 1939. Also during early September, a Ministry of Information (MOI) was brought into being. As in Germany, film and radio were considered highly important and divisions within the Ministry were assigned to those media. Graphic design activity was placed in the Home Publicity Division. The first morale posters issued by the MOI during September 1939 were not successful. Contentious copywriting featured on all three posters forming a campaign series. The copy was written by A. P. Waterfield, Deputy Director-General of the MOI. Mass Observation, which had been formed in 1937 as Britain's first public opinion body, discovered that these posters, in particular 'Your Courage, your Cheerfulness, will Bring us Victory', were not popular. The 'us' was interpreted as meaning making sacrifices for government ends. *The Times* also considered this poster to be patronizing. Gradually, as the months progressed, a more down-to-earth level of communication was established. A popular series for the 1940 'Careless Talk Costs Lives' campaign was designed by Fougasse (the pseudonym for the humorous artist Cyril Kenneth Bird).

The Director-General of the MOI between August and December 1940 was Frank Pick. It was Pick who probably realized the potential of public exhibitions, and the MOI established an Exhibitions Branch shortly before his resignation (he died on 7 November 1941). In charge of the Exhibitions Branch was Milner Gray. The use of outside sites such as the booking hall at Charing Cross Underground Station created the opportunity for several graphic designers to show their skills. These included F. H. K. Henrion, Peter Ray, Charles Hasler, George Him and Jan Le Witt. Milner Gray left the Exhibitions Division (as it had grown to) in 1943. On the 1 January 1943 Gray became instrumental in founding the Design Research Unit, later to become a major British design group.

September 1940 saw the victory of the Royal Air Force over the German Luftwaffe. Heroic images of pilots now featured on posters. On the ground, the women of the Women's Auxiliary Air Force (WAAF) had played a major role during the Battle of Britain. Jonathan Foss' poster 'Serve in the WAAF with the Men who Fly', shows a resolute pilot standing side by side with a young woman. This was executed by Foss when he was employed as 'Official Layout Man' in the Public Relations Department of the Air Ministry, and in this capacity he produced over sixty items of publicity material as the war progressed. Foss was one of the generation of British designers influenced by A. M. Cassandre.

As the war in Europe entered its final stage, it was foreseen that post-war Britain would have to export more in order to survive economically. The Council of Industrial Design was created in December 1944 in order to deal with this new emphasis. Problems of reconstruction would also make demands on Britain's industrial potential as returning servicemen would expect better housing, welfare and medical care. Among the health concerns existing in 1944 were venereal disease (which had risen by 139 per cent over the figures for the last year of peacetime) and the need to immunize babies against diphtheria.

After six weary years peace had returned. One of the poster copylines used by the Labour Party in the election had been 'Win the Peace'. Aircraft factories now produced prefabricated single storey houses ('prefabs') and people grew food on every available piece of bombed land. Food and clothing remained 'on the ration' (with some items it was even more severe than in wartime). The famous wartime slogan, 'Britain Can Take It!' now became paraphrased as 'Britain Can Make It!', the theme for an exhibition arranged by the Council of Industrial Design at the Victoria and Albert Museum in 1946.

Much wartime graphic design had used pictographic imagery, largely through the influence of Otto and Marie Neurath's Isotype movement. The Isotype Institute provided graphic diagrams for *Future Books*, a series devoted to current issues and published from the Autumn of 1945 for about a year. The art editor was George Adams (1905-1983), who as Georg Telcher had been a student of Johannes Itten at the Bauhaus.

In 1947, Allen Lane invited Jan Tschichold to create a new house style for Penguin Books. Current publications about typography were *Soldiers of Lead* (a guide to improve printed matter for local organizers of the Labour Party) and the magazine *Typographica*, edited by Herbert Spencer.

### The United States

Official US Government posters were notable for featuring the talents of America's best graphic artists. *Norman Rockwell* used an actual soldier behind a machine gun as a model for his poster issued as 'Let's give him Enough and On Time'. Rockwell had made his name working for *The Saturday Evening Post* and his paintings of *The Four Freedoms* were printed in the *Post*. Such was the demand, they were immediately reprinted. The US Government then had versions issued as posters for war bond purchasing drives. Eventually, the OWI distributed them overseas. Another artist was *Ben Shahn*. Shahn worked in the Graphics Division of the OWI. Surprisingly, the OWI only issued two of his poster designs, these being 'This is Nazi Brutality' and 'We French Workers Warn You…Defeat Means Slavery, Starvation, Death' (both 1942). A colleague of Shahn's at the Graphics Division was the social realist painter Bernard Perlin. He later designed

---

The War Office also had its own Public Relations Department. In June 1941 a soldier named Abram Games was posted there. In peacetime Games had worked as a freelance graphic designer and produced posters for the General Post Office and Shell-Mex BP Limited. His first War Office work was a poster asking for volunteers from serving soldiers to join the Royal Armoured Corps (he also designed the Corps' badge). However, Games felt that the Army could improve its dissemination of instructional and educational material by modern methods of graphic design, and this idea found official favour. In 1941 the veteran railway poster designer Frank Newbould (1887–1951) joined Games at the War Office as a civilian graphic designer.

The entry of the United States into the war, after the Japanese attack on Pearl Harbor on 7 December 1941, brought a further theme of allied unity into publicity. A branch of the United States Office of War Information (OWI) was established in London. In 1942 Milner Gray designed the *America Marches* exhibition for the MOI. During 1942 American service personnel flowed into Britain. In order to familiarize Americans with the British way of life, the MOI issued its booklet, *Welcome*!

*'Join the ATS', Abram Games for the War Office, Britain, 1941.*

REMEMBER DEC. 7th!

# INTRODUCTION

posters for the US Treasury Fourth War Loan. As in Britain, artists who had gained fame in the First World War tried to make a contribution, but graphic styles and tastes had changed. Typical of this category was the work of James Montgomery Flagg (1877–1960), who continued his famous Uncle Sam theme. The posters of the OWI and most other official departments were normally printed by the US Government Printing Office. They were the finest produced posters of the war.

During the war years the United States provided a sanctuary for many leading figures in the art world. The painter Mondrian arrived in 1940. Moholy-Nagy was teaching at the Chicago School of Design (the successor to the Bauhaus and later in the war to be renamed the Institute of Design). A fellow Hungarian and colleague of Moholy-Nagy at Chicago was Gyorgy Kepes. His influential book on design, *The Language of Vision*, was published in 1944.

Two famous poster artists who had made their reputations in Europe were living in New York. In 1940 E. McKnight Kauffer returned from Britain. However, his war poster output was small, comprising several designs for Greek war relief and the US treasury in 1944. As previously mentioned, Jean Carlu had been responsible for the *France at War* display at the 1940 New York World Fair. The fall of France found him stranded in America and he volunteered his services for the Free French cause. His poster 'America's Answer! PRODUCTION' was carried out for the Division of Information, US Office of Emergency Management, just before the entry of the United States into the war. He was later graphic adviser to the OWI.

The 1940s was an era when many young designers resumed or started their careers. In 1945 Herb Lubalin was appointed Creative Director and Vice-President of Sudler & Hennessey (also directing their graphic design office of Sudler, Hennessey & Lubalin). Louis Danziger returned from military service in 1945. After a period of study with Alvin Lustig, he became a designer at *Esquire* magazine in 1948. A year later he started his own practice in Los Angeles. Henry Wolf, who had been born in Vienna and had arrived in New York via Paris in 1941, was also one of the graphic designers who had served in the American armed forces.

### The Soviet Union

In September 1941 the British Minister of Supply, Lord Beaverbrook, accompanied by an American mission under Averell Harriman, arrived in Moscow to ascertain the military equipment needs of Russia. Beaverbrook returned with a selection of Soviet posters, including several by the Kukryniksi group (the artists Mikhail Vasilievich Kuprianov, Porfiry Mikitovich Krylov and Nikołai

*'May the courageous example of our great predecessors inspire you in the war', Victor Ivanov and Olga Burova for USSR Official, 1942.*

Alexandrovich Sokolov). The MOI subsequently issued these as part of its Anglo-Soviet common anti-Nazi war drive.

Russia had been a pioneer in the use of film for propaganda purposes. Eisenstein's historically based epics, such as *Alexander Nevsky* (1938), would provide morale-raising models for the films *Henry V* (1944) and *Kolberg* (1944). Historicism also formed a major ingredient for Soviet wartime posters, with reference being made to Alexander Nevsky's victory over the Knights of the Teutonic Order (Lake Pripus 1242) and the French attack on Russia in 1812.

Many designs were produced by a stencil technique (a feature of Kukryniksi posters). They also appeared in very large sizes for street display purposes. Heroic copy spurred the population on in their great patriotic struggle against 'the Fascist beast'.

### France

Jean Carlu's American poster, 'France Forever', proudly shows the Cross of Lorraine and the motto *Liberté Egalité Fraternité*. In London, General de Gaulle issued his famous proclamation, 'A Tous les Français!' ('To all Frenchmen!'). A repeat of the famous First World War call, *On les Aura!* ('Let them have it!') also appeared on a poster showing a French soldier with his British and American comrades in arms.

Vichy printed matter centred around images of Marshal Pétain, the hero of the Battle of Verdun during the First World War. His portrait was placed in all school classrooms and the authorities endeavoured to create the propaganda idea of Pétain having saved France in her desperate hour of need. Anti-Communism was also a strong theme for posters, but support for the Vichy régime declined as more French workers were transported to work in Germany.

*'We French workers warn you . . . defeat means slavery, starvation and death', Ben Shahn for OWI, US, 1942.*

*'Remember Dec 7th!', Bernard Perlin for OWI, US, 1942.*

1 *Apéro Tonique Virtus, tonic water aperitif, Belgium, c.1940.* 2 *Forza hazel nut milk chocolate bar wrapper, France, c.1949.* 3 *Lucky Strike pack, Raymond Loewy, US, 1940.* 4 *Drene shampoo, colour printed advertisement, Britain, 1948.* 5 *Calypso sweets wrapper, France, c.1940.*

# ADVERTISEMENTS

1

On ne trouve pas partout
des parapluies ABRI,
mais une belle poignée
est toujours signée

0612

JEAN GRŒNÉ
PARIS

EN VENTE DANS LES MAGASINS ÉLÉGANTS ET DE BON TON

2

le rouge baiser
permet le baiser

3

BANDIT

DE
ROBERT
PIGUET

6

Signs for Safety

NORTH
BRITISH

NORTH BRITISH

TYRES FOR SAFETY & LONG SERVICE

4

4 couleurs

JIF
PANTA
A 4 MINES DE COULEUR

5

**1** *Clothing by JIL, magazine advertisement, R.Blonde, France, 1947.* **2** *Jean Groene, advertisement, Draeger, France, c.1947.* **3** *'Le Rouge Baiser', advertisement, France, 1949.* **4** *North British tyre advertisement, Britain, 1947.* **5** *Jif, advertisement, R.Poquin, France, 1946.* **6** *Bandit nail polish, France, c.1947.*

# POSTERS

1

2

3

4

5

*1 'Women of Britain come into the factories', poster, Philip Zec, Britain, c.1942. 2 Poster for the Dutch Government in exile, Britain, 1944. 3 F.H.K.Henrion as part of anti-VD campaign, Britain, 1943-44. 4 Ben Shahn, US, 1942. 5 Sticker for government telephone apparatus, Britain, 1941.*

6

**6** *Poster, Sevek, Britain, 1945.*
**7** *Kukriniksky (Mikail Vasilievich, Porfiry Mikitovich Krylov and Nikolai Sokolov), USSR (printed in Britain), 1941.*

# POSTERS

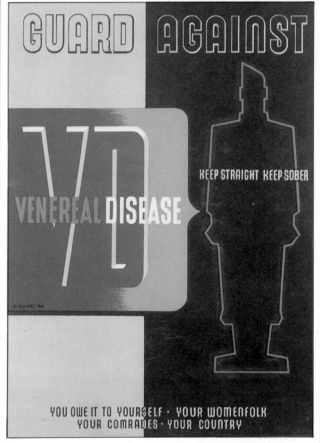

**3**

1 *Poster issued by the Free French in London, France, 1940s.* 2 *Abram Games for the War Office, Britain, c.1942.* 3 *Poster, Abram Games for War Office, Britain, 1945 General Election.* 4 *F.H.K.Henrion for US Office of War Information, issued worldwide, 1943.*

**1**

**2**

**6**

5 *Steven Dohanos for the Office of War Information, US, 1944.* 6 *Blackout poster, G.R.Morris, National Safety First Association, Britain, c.1940.*

**4**

**5**

7 Issued by USSR Official, c.1943. 8 Poster, Abram Games for the War Office, 1945 re-issue from 1942. 9 Photogravure reproduction of R.Gerbard Zill painting, Germany, 1943. 10 Ministry of Information poster, Britain, September 1940. 11 Poster issued by the Dutch Government in exile, c.1941.

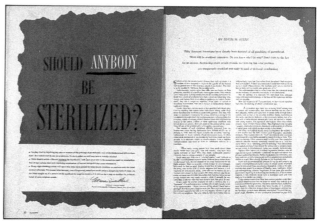

1 *Woman's Home Companion, cover, US, March 1949.*
2 *Spread from Woman's Home Companion, US, September 1948.* 3 *Spread from Woman's Home companion, US, April 1949.* 4 *Spread from Woman's Home Companion, US, April 1949.*

**Vogue**

**Vogue**

PRACTICAL
FASHIONS
AND
ACCESSORIES
•
NOVEMBER 1942 (11)
INCLUDING
VOGUE PATTERN BOOK
PRICE 3/-
THE CONDÉ NAST PUBLICATIONS LTD.
1 NEW BOND STREET, LONDON, W.1

Sp
Fash
in
Paris a
Londo

APRIL, 1946
PRICE 3/-
INCLUDING
VOGUE PATTERN BOOK
THE CONDÉ NAST PUBLICATIONS LTD.

**5** *Vogue. Britain, April 1946.*
**6** *Vogue, Britain, 1942.*

**5**

**6**

1 *Ladies' Home Journal, cover by Leslie Gill, US, 1947.*
2 *Spread from Ladies' Home Journal, US, 1947.* 3 *Page from Ladies' Home Journal, US, 1947.* 4 *Interior design article, Ladies' Home Journal, US, 1947.*

**7**

**5**

**6**

**8**

**5** *The Saturday Evening Post,* cover by Steven Dohanos, US, 1946. **6** *This Week magazine — The Indianapolis Star,* cover by Victor de Palma, US, 1946. **7** *Spread from* *Ladies' Home Journal, US, March 1947.* **8** *Spread from Woman's Home Companion, US, March 1949.*

# BOOKS

*Transformation*

FUTURE BOOKS

VOL IV

5 s. net

**1**

**2**

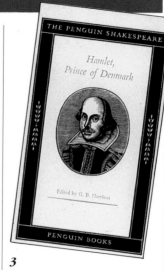

**3**

*Scripts' by Alfred Fairbanks, Jan Tschichold, Penguin Books, Britain, 1949.* **3** *Hamlet, The Penguin Shakespeare, Britain.*

**4** *'A Prospect of Wales' by Kenneth Rowntree and G.Jones, Penguin Books Ltd, Britain, 1948.*

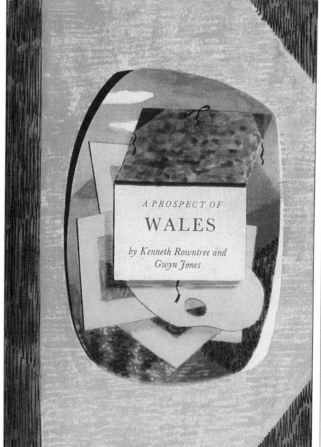

**1** *Future Books: Transformations Vol IV, George Adams, published by Collins, Britain, 1946.* **2** *'A Book of*

**4**

# SYMBOLS AND TRADEMARKS

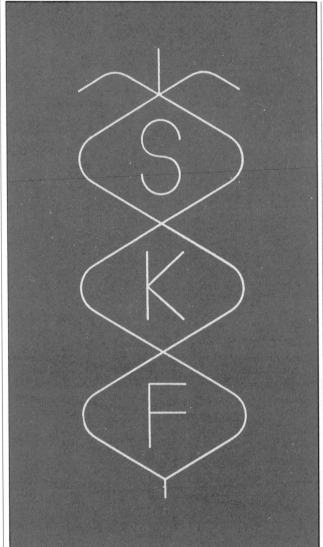

3

XIVTH OLYMPIAD 1948

4

5

**1** Smith, Kline and French trademark, Paul Rand, US, 1945. **2** Television service symbol, Abram Games, Britain, c.1949-1950. **3** Eagle drawing pencils logo, Britain, 1949-1950. **4** Winsor & Newton Ltd, logo, Britain, 1949-50. **5** XIVth Olympiad symbol, Wembley, Britain, 1948. **6** CC41 Utility symbol for furniture, Britain, 1941.

6

# NEWSPAPERS

## The Daily Telegraph and Morning Post

No. 27,763    LONDON, WEDNESDAY, JUNE 7, 1944    Printed in London and Manchester    PRICE 1½d.

4 A.M.

### ALLIED INVASION TROOPS SEVERAL MILES INTO FRANCE

#### FIGHTING IN CAEN: 10,000 TONS OF BOMBS BLASTED WAY

**NAVY'S FIRST INVASION TASK COMPLETED**

4,000 Ships Taken Across Channel

MINE - SWEEPING BY 10,000 MEN

Coastal Batteries Silenced

**"MANY DIFFICULTIES AND DANGERS BEHIND US"**

Mr. CHURCHILL REPORTS INITIAL PROGRESS 'SATISFACTORY'

**WATCHED NAVY POUND FRENCH COAST**

NO NAZI FIGHTERS OR HEAVY FLAK

**U.S. NAVY LOST ONLY 3 SHIPS**

---

THE TIMES · WEDNESDAY JUNE 5 1940

### LEAVING DUNKIRK: "OUT OF THE JAWS OF DEATH"

THE EMBARKATION FROM THE DUNES.

BOARDING A DESTROYER.—Troops of the British Expeditionary Force on the pier at Dunkirk just about to board a destroyer.

REACHING A DESTROYER.

WAITING ON THE DUNES.—British troops on a beach near Dunkirk forming into long winding queues ready to take their turn to board small boats which took them to larger vessels.

COMRADES IN ARMS.—French troops from the Army commanded by General Prioux, who fought gallantly in the region of Dunkirk, seen on their arrival at a British port yesterday.

**BROADCASTING**

A SYMPHONY CONCERT

HOME SERVICE

**THE ESTATE MARKET**

NOTTINGHAM LAND

**ST. JOHN AMBULANCE BRIGADE**

**THE TIMES CROSSWORD PUZZLE No. 3,209**

WILLS'S Gold Flake WIN ON QUALITY

SAVE FOR SALVAGE

HERE'S LUCK

A noble spirit, full of years, whose rare bouquet and lingering after-glow have won the verdict : 'fine as a fine liqueur'. WHITE HORSE

**1** *The Times, back page, Britain, June 5, 1940.* **2** *The Daily Telegraph, Britain, June 7, 1944.*

# INFORMATION DESIGN

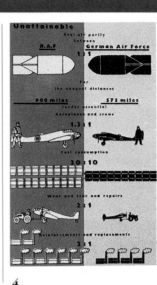

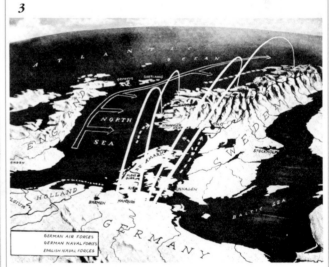

OFFICIAL INSTRUCTIONS ISSUED BY THE MINISTRY OF HOME SECURITY

## GAS ATTACK

### HOW TO PUT ON YOUR GAS MASK

Always keep your gas mask with you – day and night. Learn to put it on quickly. Practise wearing it.

1. Hold your breath.    2. Hold mask in front of face, with thumbs inside straps.
3. Thrust chin well forward into mask, pull straps over head as far as they will go.
4. Run finger round face-piece taking care head-straps are not twisted.

### IF THE GAS RATTLES SOUND

1. Hold your breath. Put on mask wherever you are. Close window.

2. If out of doors, take off hat, put on your mask. Turn up collar.

3. Put on gloves or keep hands in pockets. Take cover in nearest building.

### IF YOU GET GASSED

**BY VAPOUR GAS**   Keep your gas mask on even if you feel discomfort
If discomfort continues go to First Aid Post

**BY LIQUID or BLISTER GAS**

| 1 | 2 | 3 | 4 |
|---|---|---|---|
| Dab, but *don't rub* the splash with handkerchief. Then destroy handkerchief. | Rub No. 2 Ointment well into place. *(Buy a 6d. jar now from any chemist).* In emergency chemists supply Bleach Cream free. | If you can't get Ointment or Cream within 5 minutes wash place with soap and warm water | Take off at once any garment splashed with gas. |

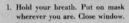
PRINTED FOR H.M. STATIONERY OFFICE BY POSH & CROSS LTD., LONDON. (51/304.)

**1**

---

867

## A TOUS LES FRANÇAIS

*La France a perdu une bataille!*
*Mais la France n'a pas perdu la guerre!*

Des gouvernants de rencontre ont pu capituler, cédant à la panique, oubliant l'honneur, livrant le pays à la servitude. Cependant, rien n'est perdu!

Rien n'est perdu, parce que cette guerre est une guerre mondiale. Dans l'univers libre, des forces immenses n'ont pas encore donné. Un jour, ces forces écraseront l'ennemi. Il faut que la France, ce jour-la, soit présente à la victoire. Alors, elle retrouvera sa liberté et sa grandeur. Tel est mon but, mon seul but!

Voilà pourquoi je convie tous les Francais, où qu'ils se trouvent, à s'unir à moi dans l'action, dans le sacrifice et dans l'espérance.

Notre patrie est en péril de mort.
Luttons tous pour la sauver!

## VIVE LA FRANCE !

GÉNÉRAL DE GAULLE

QUARTIER-GÉNÉRAL,
4, CARLTON GARDENS,
LONDON, S.W.1.

**2**

**1** *'Gas attack . . .', Ministry of Home Security poster, Britain, c.1939.* **2** *General de Gaulle's proclamation, issued by the Free French in London, c.1942.*

# TYPOGRAPHY

ABCDEFGHIJKLM
NOPQRSTUVWXYZ
1234567890

**1** *Profil, Eugen and Max Lenz, Haas, 1946.*

ABCDEFGHIJKLMNOPQRSTUVWXYZ&
abcdefghijklmnopqrstuvwxyz

**2** *Greenwich, William E. Fink, Ludlow, 1940.*

# BANK NOTES

**1** *Chinese bank note, 1886-1946.* **2** *100 franc note, France, 1940s.* **3** *5 franc note, France, 1940s.* **4** *5 franc note, France, 1940s.*

*Dunlop rubber advertisement, Festival of Britain catalogue, Britain, 1951.*

# CHAPTER · FOUR

# 1950
## TO
# 1959

# INTRODUCTION

The 1950s solidified the economic and ideological division between the Western capitalist way of life and the Eastern socialist way of life. America's lead in Western commercialism gave rise to a new consumer society. The American Dream of 'Mom, home and apple pie' expanded to include high living standards, 'mod cons', suburbia and a car in every garage. America's lifestyle, products and ideas were copied all over the world, spread by advertising, pop music, Hollywood films and television. A product of the expanding consumer society was the new concept of the 'teenager' or youth market, symbolized by teen idols such as Elvis Presley and James Dean and exported worldwide. Needless to say, with the creation of new markets and the boom in consumerism, the advertising and entertainment media had never had it so good.

Television overtook film and radio and became the primary broadcasting medium in America and Britain, and gradually took hold in other countries. It was to assume an increasingly important role in people's lives as a carrier of entertainment and advertising, as well as news and politics. Presidential elections were to receive nationwide TV coverage in America by the end of the 1950s, and Vietnam would become the first televized war in the 1960s.

The 1950s also marked the beginning of the Nuclear Age. With the use of the atom bomb on Nagasaki and Hiroshima in 1945 and the growing use of jet fighter technology in the Korean War in the early 1950s, world demolition had become a real possibility. Consequently the Cold War discussion arena took on increasing importance, with the United Nations as its base. 'The Bomb' became the symbol of world paranoia, which increased as the products of the Nuclear Age multiplied to include nuclear power stations, ships, submarines, bomb testing and air raid warning tests and shelters. The Nuclear Arms Race had begun – and with it the Campaign for Nuclear Disarmament, founded in Britain in 1958 by Bertrand Russell and Canon John Collins. As the Arms Race escalated, so did public fear for the future. World peace and nuclear disarmament became strong global issues in the following decades.

### The United States

With a prosperous expanding economy and commercialism riding high, America evolved a consumer society bound to uphold the American Dream, or the American way of life. Essential aspects of this luxurious dream were the American home, equipped with all modern conveniences, and the American car (the bigger the car, the better).

As a result, advertising of commercial domestic products embarked on a golden decade in the 1950s. The major advertisers included: for cars – General Motors (Chevrolet, Buick, Cadillac etc.), Ford Motor Company, Chrysler Corporation; for soaps and/or foods – Procter & Gamble, General Foods, Colgate-Palmolive; for household ap-

pliances and public utilities – General Electric, RCA and Westinghouse.

More manufacturers advertised in magazines than in any other media. Most important were the three mass-circulation 'general editorial' magazines – *Life, Saturday Evening Post* and *Look* – which were estimated to reach nearly two-thirds of the households in America. And there was an abundance of ad-carrying magazines aimed at major groups within the population (men or women, urban or rural) or specialist audiences. This second category included magazines like *Fortune* business magazine and *Holiday* leisure magazine, both of which commissioned well-known graphic artists and illustrators like Paul Rand, Robert Weaver and Harvey Schmidt.

Madison Avenue became the advertising centre of the world, and half of American industry's advertising budget was spent by Madison Avenue agencies. At the 'top of the heap' (agency-wise) were J. Walter Thompson, McCann-Erickson, Young & Rubicam and Batten, Barton, Durstine & Osborn (BBDO). (All had received their post-war growth injection around 1947.) Other well-known agencies of the time were N.W. Ayer & Son, Benton & Bowles, Ted Bates & Company and Foote, Cone & Belding. Just as a matter of interest, various Bauhaus emigrés from the 1930s and 1940s, such as Herbert Bayer, were now part of the New York commercial art and advertising establishment.

The 1950s saw the creation of important design practices under 'big names' such as Charles Eames, Raymond Loewy, George Nelson and Henry Dreyfuss. These were large firms centred around one person – not partnerships or teams of associates – and the big names involved were usually industrial designers who worked across a broad spectrum of product design, furniture, graphics and even film.

Other important designers of the period included Paul Rand, William Golden, Robert Brownjohn, Henry Wolf and Saul Bass. Paul Rand, having produced much of the best advertising work of the 1940s, designed the graphics for the IBM corporate identity in the 1950s, and the Westinghouse identity later in the 1960s. William Golden was the Director of Design at CBS (radio and television) and designed the CBS corporate identity, including the famous CBS 'eye' symbol. Robert Brownjohn, master of the visual pun, joined the partnership of Brownjohn, Geismar and Chermayeff in 1957, which became one of New York's most innovative graphic design groups and had a great influence on young designers in the 1960s. Brownjohn left the United States for England in 1960. Henry Wolf was made art director of *Esquire* magazine in 1952 and art director of *Harper's Bazaar* in 1958. Wolf was responsible for numerous magazine cover designs and advertisements, and broke the slick commercial art mould by commissioning artists (such as Ben Shahn) who were unfamiliar to magazine work. Saul Bass worked in both 3-D and graphic design, and made a special contribution in film – particularly the design of

*The original IBM logotype (c.1945) and the 1955 redesign, Paul Rand, US.*

*1 Oldsmobile advertisement, US, 1959.*

90

NINETY-EIGHT HOLIDAY SPORTSEDAN

**Every 1959 Oldsmobile** has the smart new "Linear Look"—trim, light, wide-open, spacious! Inside and out it's aglow with bright ideas—safer brakes, improved visibility, smoother ride, more luggage room. Yes, and a brand-new Rocket Engine, too! An engine that is incredibly smooth, the most efficient Rocket yet. Think a moment. Isn't it time to step up to an Olds—*acknowledged leader in the medium price class!* Talk it over with your local quality dealer.

OLDSMOBILE DIVISION,
GENERAL MOTORS CORPORATION

## OLDSMOBILE FOR '59

DYNAMIC 88 HOLIDAY SCENICOUPE

1

credit titles, which he elevated into an art in itself. His most famous collaborations were with film-makers Otto Preminger and Alfred Hitchcock in the late 1950s and early 1960s.

The concept of the 'teenager' was an American invention of the 1950s and youth culture quickly became one of the hottest markets around. Advertising proliferated for teen-orientated products such as hi-fi records, motorcycles, hair cosmetics, make-up and 'fads' like the hula hoop. Teenage magazines and teenage television reinforced All-American youth stereotypes such as the clean-cut home-town guy (Tab Hunter, Ricky Nelson, Rock Hudson) and the girl-next-door (Sandra Dee, Doris Day). Rock'n'roll, on the other hand, presented youth culture with better options – sex, rebellion and being misunderstood. And it offered idols to worship in the form of Elvis Presley, Buddy Holly, Jerry Lee Lewis, and other rock stars. Rock'n'roll imagery appeared on record sleeves, sheet music, magazines, posters, clothes and paraphernalia (badges etc).

Hollywood also influenced graphic imagery and advertising. Sex and glamour was provided by Marilyn Monroe and Liz Taylor, sex and rebellious anger by Marlon Brando and James Dean. In the late 1950s and early 1960s clean, home-town romance was epitomized by the Doris Day/Rock Hudson team in films such as *Pillow Talk*. All the screen idols were displayed for adoration on posters, publicity shots and in fan magazines. But despite all marketing efforts, the film industry was still fighting for its life against the new arrival – television.

The American Dream soon demanded that each home should have a 'TV'. Children's TV programmes such as *The Lone Ranger* and *Davy Crockett* yielded child consumer products such as Davy Crockett's 'coon-hat'. For teenagers there was *Dick Clark's American Bandstand* and *77 Sunset Strip*. And for Mom and Dad, quiz shows, soap operas and situation comedy series both entertained and reinforced the rock-solid values of American family-life and the commercial establishment, both of which would come under heavy attack from youth culture in the 1960s.

### Britain

The early 1950s were a time of food and clothing rationing for Britain. Power and material restrictions also extended into many other aspects of everyday activity. Outdoor advertising provided some relief in a landscape still desolate with bomb sites and disused air raid shelters. Paper shortages after the war had resulted in walls having painted advertisements and the walls of corner shops were crammed with enamel signs advertising soft drinks or cigarettes with catchy slogans such as 'Player's Please'. The demand for public transport had never been greater. Tram, bus and trolleybus advertising spaces were eagerly booked by the leading brands of the day.

Gradually Government controls were lifted (newsprint remained rationed until as late as 1956). In 1954 food

*'Room at the Top' by John Braine, cover by Hans Schmoller, Penguin Books Ltd, Britain, 1959.*

rationing ended and during the same year the abolition of hire purchase controls opened the doors to the creation of a consumer society. The time was right for the introduction of commercial television. Television broadcasts financed through advertising begain in September 1955. Programme sponsorship was forbidden. The effect of commercial television on press advertising was immediate, and by the end of the decade three national weekly magazines had ceased publication, the best-known being *Picture Post* which closed in 1957.

The Guinness illuminated clock at Piccadilly Circus had been one of the advertising sites switched on again in 1949 and soon Benson's creative staff had thought up new ideas for the 'Guinness for Strength' campaign. In 1951 Wilk (Dick Wilkinson) delighted the passer-by in the street with his Guinness poster showing a workman lifting up a steamroller. The jet age was alluded to with Gilroy's poster showing a fly-past of toucans balancing glasses of the world famous stout on their beaks!

Shell's expertise in the field of public relations was represented by their press and magazine advertising. A popular series was *Flowers of the Countryside* (1954), featuring paintings by Edith and Roland Hilder. The theme of nature was continued by *Birds and Beasts* (1955), also by Roland Hilder with Maurice Wilson. The quiet restrained advertising message they contained made the broadsheet versions acceptable to schoolteachers, who placed them in prominent positions in many British classrooms.

The Festival of Britain (1951) was a nationwide event. Its principal site was on the South Bank of the Thames near County Hall. Rubble left from the London 'Blitz' was used to reclaim land from the Thames and much sub-standard housing was cleared. Although the centenary of the 1851 Great Exhibition was used to provide a commemorative *raison d'etre*, the 1951 Festival was in reality a morale-raising inspiration for post-war recovery. Many designers who had worked in the various divisions of the wartime MOI would take a major role in its realization. Abram Games devised the Festival symbol and a version of it for use on postage stamps. James Holland, James Gardner, Beverley Pick and F.H.K. Henrion would all design displays in the various pavilions. Milner Gray and Robin Day designed the South Bank outdoor sign system.

In terms of graphic design the big influence of the Festival came through the Typography Panel, under its Chairman Charles Hasler. The Festival *Specimen Book* for lettering included revivals of early nineteenth century display typefaces cut by Figgins, Thorne and Austin. The graphic eclecticism of the Festival of Britain 'style' permeated into art schools. Soon art students started to design posters which recalled nineteenth century theatre bills. The popularity of New Orleans jazz found expression in student dance posters using Egyptian typefaces!

Harold F. Hutchinson was now Publicity Officer to London Transport. The posters of John Minton, Edward Bawden, Abram Games, Tom Eckersley, and F.H.K. Henrion carried on the Underground public art tradition.

A great influence on graphic design, and typography in particular, was Herbert Spencer. In the immediate post-war years Spencer worked for London Typographical Designers, a design group which had been established by a group of ex-MOI graphic designers. He followed in Tschichold's footsteps by designing the *Penrose Annual* in 1949. He began his association with Lund Humpries in 1950, when he was appointed their consultant art director.

Typographers working in publishing fields were Hans Schmoller (Penguin Books), Ruari McLean and John Lewis (typographic adviser to the Ipswich printers W.S. Cowell).

Among the graphic designers who had arrived in Britain during the 1930s were Hans Schleger (1898-1976) and F.H.K. Henrion. Both men had largely established their reputations as poster designers. In 1953 Schleger decided to broaden his activities and formed his own design group, Hans Schleger Associates. Among the corporate design undertaken was for London Transport, the Mac Fisheries provisions chain and the John Lewis Partnership. F.H.K. Henrion also decided to develop along the same path and Henrion Design Associates came into being. Schleger and Henrion both taught at the Royal College of Art.

## Italy

Italian post-war recovery was largely helped by Marshall Aid and the adaption of its manufacturing industry to new markets. Wartime factories were turned over to the production of economy road vehicles such as the motor scooter, which became a symbol of the 1950s.

Fiat, Olivetti and Pirelli all had long traditions of design patronage. Giovanni Pintori entered the Publicity Department of Olivetti in 1936. He became Head of Graphic Design in 1950 and much of the famous advertising which appeared during the following decade came from his hand.

Several graphic designers who had been born outside Italy worked in Milan. These included Swiss-born Max Huber, who after training at the Zurich Kunstgewerbeschule, joined the Studio Boggeri in 1940. During the 1950s he freelanced. Another Swiss was Walter Balmer, who

*Olivetti Lexikon Elettrica*
*advertisement, Italy, 1957.*

joined Olivetti as an in-house graphic designer in 1956. Bob Noorda, born in Amsterdam, freelanced for many major companies including Philips, Alfa Romeo and Pirelli. He became Art Director of Pirelli in 1961. The principal designers working for Studio Boggeri were René Martinelli and Aldo Calabresi.

## Poland

The Polish poster has received international acclaim since the 1930s. As in other Eastern European countries, the economic and political system in Poland

Henryk Tomaszewski has remained the great master of Polish poster design and has influenced many students (both Polish and otherwise) during his years as Professor at the Academy of Fine Arts in Warsaw. Jan Lenica, another great artist, was renowned not only for posters, but also satirical cartoons and animated films. Roman Cieslewicz, who studied poster art at the Academy in Cracow, was at this time representative of a younger generation of poster artists heavily influenced by Tomaszewski. Like Lenica, Cieslewicz left Poland to live in France in the early 1960s, and became an important member of the new avant-garde of the 1970s and 1980s.

diminished the requirement for commercial advertising. Freed from a commercial role, the Polish poster applied itself to cultural and political themes and achieved world recognition in the 1950s through poster artists such as Henryk Tomaszewski, Jan Lenica and Roman Cieslewicz. The main centres for poster design were the capital city of Warsaw and, to a lesser extent, Poznan and Cracow. Other important activities for Poland's graphic artists were book illustration, exhibition design and film.

Much of Poland's poster art of the 1950s was connected to film, for Poland was acknowledged as a leading film-making nation. Many graphic artists worked on films themselves – for example, Walerian Borowczyk joined with Jan Lenica to make the animated film *Once Upon a Time*, which won several international awards in 1957/58.

# PACKAGING

February, 1954          *Ideal Home*

*Lovingly sprinkle these flakes of superb chocolate on to very warm milk... lightly stir... the richness, the perfection of true chocolate instantly awaits you! Surely no more luxurious, no more truly well-bred drink than Cadbury's Cup Chocolate exists!*

**2/3d a half-pound**

CADBURY'S **CUP** CHOCOLATE

MICHEL SCHNEIDER NACHF. MERL b. ZELL-MOSEL

Mosel, Saar     und Ruwer

*ges. Zeller Schwarze Katz gesch.*

1956er

Riesling

Vinařské závody, n. p. Praha

závod 02, Praha 9-Vysočany, U vinných sklepů 145

Have a **CAPSTAN**

MEDIUM STRENGTH
**CAPSTAN**
Navy Cut
**CIGARETTES**
W. D. & H. O. WILLS.
BRISTOL & LONDON.
20 CIGARETTES

*— made to make friends*

**1** Cadbury's packaging from advertisement, Britain, 1954.    **2** Black Cat Reisling wine label, W. Germany, 1956.

94

4

Evening in Paris perfume, cologne. **37/6**

Bath cubes in Ashes of Roses, Ashes of Violets, Lavender. **3/4**

Evening in Paris perfume, bath cubes, toilet soaps. **8/9**

Evening in Paris talcum, cologne. **7/9**

BOURJOIS

5

STATE EXPRESS
555
THE BEST CIGARETTES IN THE WORLD

6

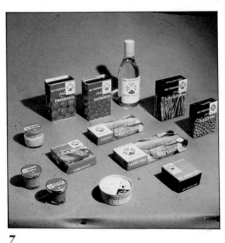

7

**3** Capstan packaging from magazine advertisement, Imperial Tobacco Company, Britain, c.1951. **4** Seita packaging with Pyrolac advertisement on box, France, c.1952. **5** Bourjois packaging from magazine advertisement, France, 1957. **6** State Express 555 packaging from magazine advertisement, Britain, c.1951. **7** MacFisheries packaging, Hans Schleger, Britain, 1954.

# ADVERTISEMENTS

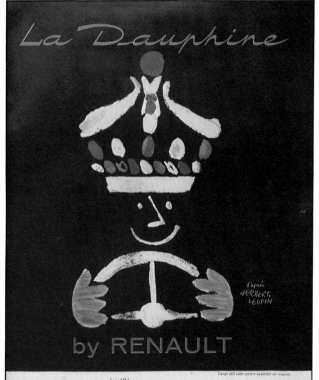

A NEW LOOK IN STYLING –
BIG POWER ADVANCES
FOR 'MINOR'
AND 'COWLEY'

Morris "Quality First" policy
leaps ahead in the new models which will be
introduced at the Motor Show, Earls Court.
Here briefly are the salient features of a range of cars
destined for an enthusiastic reception.

**1**

1 *Renault car advertisement,
Herbert Leupin, Esquire
magazine, US, 1957.*
2 *Canadian Schenley whisky
advertisement, US, 1951.*
3 *Campbell's V-8 vegetable
juice advertisement, US, 1950s.*
4 *Grumman Aircraft
advertisement, National
Geographic magazine, US,
1955.* 5 *Morris car
advertisement, Reader's Digest
magazine, 1956.*

**6** Cheer Washday detergent advertisement, US, 1953.
**7** Perrier mineral water advertisement, France, 1954.
**8** Gibbs SR toothpaste advertisement, Reader's Digest magazine, US, 1950s.

# ADVERTISEMENTS

New "Slant" in Windshield Design!

*A General Motors Value.*

*Car illustrated: Super "88" Holiday Coupé, White Sidewall Tires and DeLuxe Stainless Steel Wheel Discs optional at extra cost.*

*Vision of loveliness . . . with new "Rocket" liveliness! It's Oldsmobile's ultra-new Super "88" Holiday Coupé for 1954! Future-styled—with a new sweep-around panoramic windshield . . . 179 square inches more glass area! With a long, youthful, low-level silhouette! A dashing sports-car flair in door and fender design! Full-width cowl ventilator for fresh, clean, exhaust-free air at hood level! And future-powered—with the famous "Rocket" Engine stepped up to an exciting new 185 horsepower! Make a date to see and drive the sensational Super "88" for 1954 at your Oldsmobile dealer's!*

World's Record "Rocket"
**OLDSMOBILE**

**1**

*Cook sees better just what's cooking*

*When an Osram helps her looking!*

"There are no dark corners in *our* home. Not even in the kitchen!" Can you say that truly? Then it must be indeed a happy household. Such a blessing is the good abundant light that Osram gives. And Osram makes utmost use of the current! It's the way these lamps are made and tested. Thorough is the word. Good value. The light of your home!

**O**sram
THE WONDERFUL LIGHT

A **G.E.C.** Product · The General Electric Co. Ltd.

**2**

Duralay has a way with it—a soft, silent, luxurious way with it. You put it down under your bedroom carpeting and it soaks up the noise; the pile seems to grow deeper and thicker; and it lasts longer, years longer, protected by Duralay's floor-cushion. A sound investment-in-luxury is part of

*life with* **Duralay**
THE BEST CARPET UNDERLAY IN THE WORLD

**3**

**1** *World's 'Rocket' Oldsmobile Super '88' Holiday Coupé advertisement, Collier's, US, April 2, 1954.* **2** *Osram light bulbs, magazine advertisement, Britain, October, 1958.* **3** *Duralay, magazine advertisement, Britain, October 1958.* **4** *GEC Cosyglo, magazine advertisement, Britain, 1958.* **5** *Treadeasy Shoes, advertisement, Woman's Home Companion, US, May 1950.*

98

# Tele-warmth...for everyone!

Guests in to watch a T.V. programme? Room a bit chilly? Switch on the Cosyglo.

That will keep them comfortably warm whether they sit in front or at the sides.

For the Cosyglo throws out warmth all round — thanks to its wonderful, scientifically designed reflector

(exclusive to G.E.C.). It gives you what you really want — a high-styled modern fire,

with well-spread heat, which is a delight to look at — for £5.17.6.

See the many other G.E.C. fires from 46/-. Obtainable from your usual electrical supplier.

# Get a G.E.C. Cosyglo fire

# ADVERTISEMENTS

*1 Bic pen poster, R.Savignac, France, 1950s. 2 Band-Aid advertisement, US, 1959. 3 Nash Airflyte advertisement, US, c.1950. 4 Pirelli poster, André François, France, 1958. 5 Air France poster, R.Savignac, France, c.1950. 6 'Mind the child', road safety poster, Josef Müller-Brockmann, Switzerland, 1955. 7 Tweed Lenthéric advertisement, US, 1953. 8 Eversharp pen advertisement, US, 1950s.*

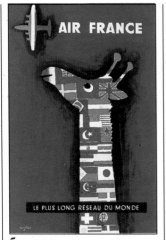

5

6

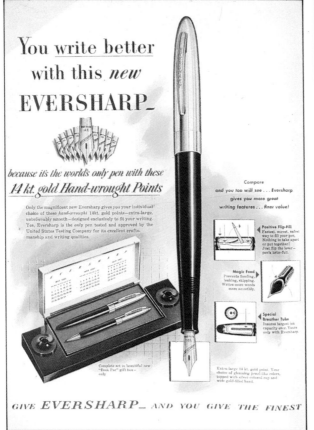

8

9

7

10

11

12

**9** Cadillac car advertisement, US, 1959. **10** CBS advertisement, William Golden, US, 1957. **11** Van Heusen tie advertisement, US, early 1950s. **12** Kia-Ora fruit drink advertisement, Britain, 1952.

# POSTERS

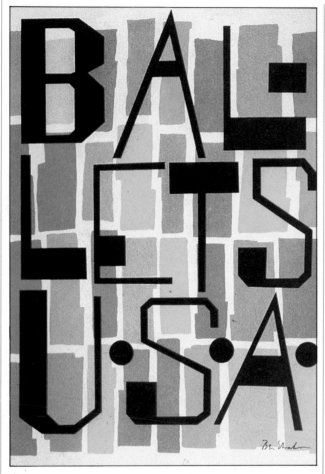

1 'Ballets USA' exhibit in London, Ben Shahn, US, 1959.
2 'Calamity Jane', film poster, US, 1953. 3 Daz detergent, R.Savignac, France, 1950s.

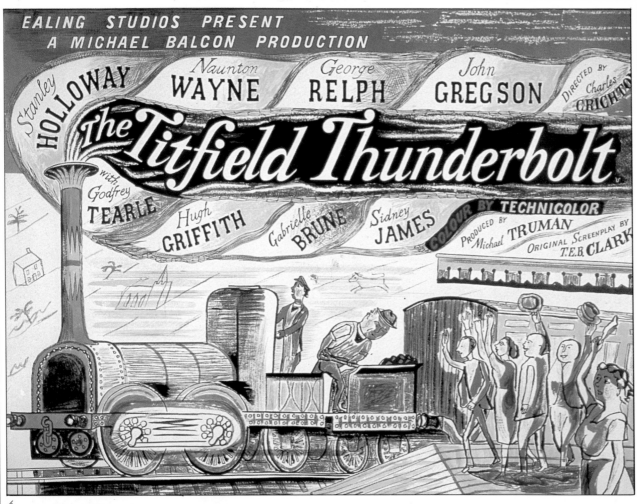

4

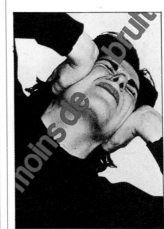

8

5

6

7

**4** *'The Titfield Thunderbolt',
film poster, Edward Bawden,
Britain, 1950s.* **5** *'Poster-ise
and Publicise — Catch the Eye
with Colour', John Bainbridge,
Britain, 1953.* **6** *Olivetti
Lexicon 80, Marcello Nizzoli,
Italy, 1950.* **7** *Woodbine
cigarette poster, Britain, 1952.*
**8** *Anti-noise poster, Josef Müller-
Brockmann, Switzerland, 1957.*

# POSTERS

# BOOKS

**1**

**2**

NON A L'AUTOROUTE RIVE GAUCHE

**3**

**1** *Theatre poster, Henryk Tomaszewski, Poland, 1958.*
**2** *Concert poster, Josef Müller-* *Brockmann, Switzerland, 1955.* **3** *Protest poster, R.Savignac, France, 1958.*

**1**

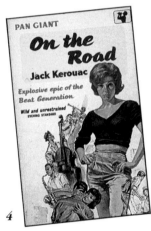

GREAT PAN

# THE DHARMA BUMS
## Jack Kerouac

Fighting, drinking, scorning convention, making wild love — zany antics of America's young Beats in their mad search for kicks

ADDS UP TO ONE HELL OF A PHILOSOPHY OF LIFE
The Listener

**3**

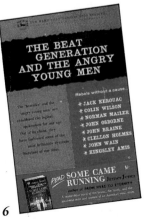

PAN GIANT

# On the Road
## Jack Kerouac

Explosive epic of the Beat Generation

Wild and unrestrained
EVENING STANDARD

**4**

BUILDING MODERN SWEDEN
BY BERTIL HULTÉN

PENGUIN BOOKS

**2**

Luigi Bartolini

## BICYCLE THIEVES

ACE BOOKS

**5**

THE BEAT GENERATION AND THE ANGRY YOUNG MEN

Rebels without a cause
★ JACK KEROUAC
★ COLIN WILSON
★ NORMAN MAILER
★ JOHN OSBORNE
★ JOHN BRAINE
★ CLELLON HOLMES
★ JOHN WAIN
★ KINGSLEY AMIS

READ SOME CAME RUNNING James Jones

**6**

**1** *Schubert music score, Penguin Books, Britain, 1950s.*
**2** *Building Modern Sweden, Penguin Books, Britain, 1950s.*
**3** *'The Dharma Bums' by Jack Kerouac, Pan Books, Britain, 1958.* **4** *'On the Road' by Jack Kerouac, Pan Books, Britain, 1958.* **5** *Back cover of 'Bicycle Thieves' by Luigi Bartolini, Ace Books, Britain, 1957.* **6** *Back cover of 'Protest: the Beat Generation and the Angry Young Men', edited by Gene Feldman and Max Gartenberg, Panther Books, 1959.*

# MAGAZINES AND JOURNALS

1

2

3

4

5

6

**1** *Picture show, Britain, 1959.*
**2** *Spread from Esquire, art director Henry Wolf, US, 1954.*
**3** *Esquire, art director Henry Wolf, US, 1954.* **4** *Ideal Home, Britain, 1954.* **5** *Picture Post, photographer Bert Hardy, Britain, 1950.* **6** *Masthead for Eagle comic, logotype by Berthold Wolpe, Britain, 1953.*
**7** *Collier's, US, 1956.*
**8** *Collier's, art director William Chessman, US, 1954.*

7

8

# MAGAZINES

REINFORCEMENTS of men and materials in a winged rocket reach the wheel-shaped space station on right. Chesley Bonestell's painting, based on authentic plans, shows men in pressurized suits floating in space and three space taxis: one leaves rocket; another nears a floating observatory; a third is at space station

BELOW: Forty miles above the earth's surface, a winged rocket jettisons its lower booster stage by parachute. The rocket—carrying man on the first stage of his greatest exploration—is equipped with wings for the return landing on the earth

## Journey Into Space

### by ARTHUR C. CLARKE, B.Sc., F.R.A.S.
*Chairman, British Interplanetary Society*

By rocket-ship to a space station: from there to the Moon and Mars.... Almost certainly man will start on his greatest adventure before the century is out. How will he do it? And what will he find in the new worlds that lie in the mysterious unexplored arch above his own familiar world?

**AN EXPERT ANSWERS THESE QUESTIONS IN A FASCINATING NEW 'ILLUSTRATED' SERIES**

SCIENTISTS now have a clear picture of the way in which the planets may be reached. It is remarkable how close the agreement is between the many experts from a dozen different countries who have studied the infant science of astronautics.

If the present rate of research continues, man will be heading through outer space, bound for the Moon and Mars, before this century comes to an end. The development of the rocket has turned fantasy into feasibility.

Instead of new continents, our children will be discovering new worlds. Many of the planets within their reach will be stranger than any regions of our own world. Some will be far colder than the Antarctic; others far hotter than the tropics. Some will have no atmospheres at all; others will be swept with storms of ammonia gas. There is no chance that, or, any of them, the crews of the first space ships will be able to leave their vessels without protection.

Yet despite many perils and hazards, men will travel out to these new worlds, across the emptiness of space, watching the earth dwindle behind them until it seems only another star. They will make these voyages for many reasons. The chief reason, of course, is scientific curiosity. There must be few people who, at some time or other, have not watched Mars glowing redly in the midnight sky or seen the electric blaze of Venus sinking into the twilight without wondering what it was like on those distant globes. Our grandchildren may know the answers.

The first spaceships will be rocket driven. Between the planets is an almost perfect vacuum—no trace of air or any other matter. Wings and propellers would be utterly useless. But the rocket, which produces thrust by the "kick" of its escaping exhaust gases, can still function perfectly under these conditions, indeed, it

OVER

**1** 'Journey into Space', article from Illustrated, Britain, July 5, 1952. **2** Illustrated, Britain, July 5, 1952. **3** Household, US, July 1953. **4** Household, US, July 1956. **5** McCall's, art editor John English, US, May 1953. **6** Page from McCall's, US, May 1953. **7** Handyman, Britain, January 1958.

May 1953

# McCall's

**25 CENTS**

5

6

**NEW DIET**

**NEW HAIRDOS**

**NEW MAKE-UP**

**NEW CLOTHES**

\*

**COMPLETE GUIDE**

**TO A PRETTIER YOU**

*How to run a happy home*

# Handyman

**This month's highlights**

**STOPPING DRAUGHTS**

**FIXING WALL PLUGS**

**CARE OF TOOLS**

**ALL ABOUT WOOD (PART TWO)**

**GUIDE TO HEATERS**

You can easily modernise
your home by fixing
wall and floor tiles . . .
read how to do it inside

7

# RECORD SLEEVES

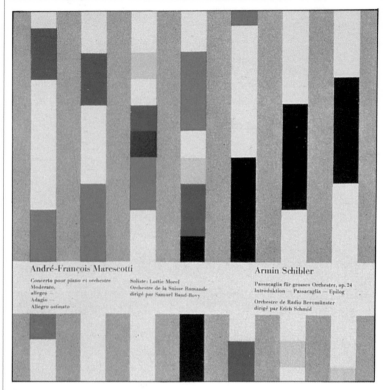

André-François Marescotti

Concerto pour piano et orchestre
Moderato,
allegro —
Adagio
Allegro ostinato

Soliste: Lottie Morel
Orchestre de la Suisse Romande
dirigé par Samuel Baud-Bovy

Armin Schibler

Passacaglia für grosses Orchester, op. 24
Introduktion — Passacaglia — Epilog
Orchestre de Radio Beromünster
dirigé par Erich Schmid

**1**

**2**

From the Sound Track of the Motion Picture

Rodgers and Hammerstein's

*Oklahoma!*

SOMETHING
THE
MUSIC
OF
ELSE !!!!
ORNETTE
COLEMAN
CONTEMPORARY
S 7551

**3**

**1** *Schweizer Komponisten, Josef Müller-Brockmann, Switzerland, 1950s.* **2** *'Oklahoma!', Rodgers and Hammerstein, Capitol Records, distributed by EMI, Britain, 1950s.* **3** *'Something Else! The Music of Ornette Coleman', Contemporary Records Inc, US, 1958.* **4** *'The King of Rumba' Xavier Cugat and his orchestra, Philips Ltd, Britain, 1950s.* **5** *'Ellington Uptown', Duke Ellington, CBS Records, US, 1953.* **6** *Mantovani and his orchestra with Rawicz and Landaner, Decca Record Company Ltd, Britain, 1960.*

Duke Ellington
and his orchestra

ELLINGTON UPTOWN

LP CBS

**5**

*Xavier Cugat*
and
his
orchestra
*The King of Rumba*

Mambo No. 8
Cerego Rosa Y
Manzano Blanco
Lisboa Antigua
Me Lo Dijo Adel
Carnival In
Uruguay
El Choclo
El Marijuano
Cuando Te
Beso Tiemblo

PHILIPS
Minigroove 33⅓
A PRODUCT OF PHILIPS ELECTRICAL LIMITED

**4**

DECCA
RECORDS

*mantovani* and his Orchestra

with *rawicz* and *landauer*

Warsaw Concerto
Serenata d'Amore
The Dream of Olwen
The Legend of the Glass Mountain
Story of Three Loves
Cornish Rhapsody

play music from the films

**6**

# SYMBOLS AND TRADEMARKS

1

2

3

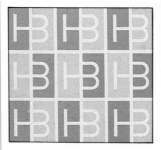

5

6

4

1 *Festival of Britain poster, symbol by Abram Games, Britain, 1951.* 2 *Logo for Harcourt Brace & Co, Paul Rand, US, 1957.* 3 *Application of HB logo, Paul Rand, US, 1957.* 4 *Logo for Consolidated Eigar Corporation, Paul Rand, US, 1959.* 5 *CBS television symbol, William Golden, US, 1950.* 6 *Design Council symbol (unused version), Hans Schleger, Britain, 1955.*

# TYPOGRAPHY

ABCDEFGHIJKLMNOPQRSTUVWXYZ
abcdefghijklmnopqrstuvwxyz
1234567890

*1 Helvetica, M.Miedinger, Haas, Germany, 1957.*

ABCDEFGHIJKLMNOPQRSTUVW
abcdefghijklmnopqrstuvwxyz
1234567890

*2 Optima, Hermann Kapf, Stempel, Germany, 1958.*

ABCDEFGHIJKLMNOPQRSTUVWXYZ
abcdefghijklmnopqrstuvwxyz
1234567890

*3 Univers, Adrian Frutiger, Deberny & Peignot, France, 1957.*

ABCDEFGHIJKLMNOPQ
RSTUVXYWZCÆŒ&

*4 Microgramma, A.Butti and A.Novarese, Nebiolo, Italy, 1952.*

ABCDEFGHIJKLMNOPQRSTUVWXYZ
1234567890

*5 Festival, Phillip Boydell, Monotype, Britain, 1951.*

THE SOCIETY OF TYPOGRAPHIC DESIGNERS

THE TYPOGRAPHER

NUMBER 13 DECEMBER 1953

*6 Typographer magazine issue 13, Britain, December 1953.*

*1 100 lire note, Italy, 1951.
2 1,000 pesetas note, Spain, 1951. 3 1,000 pesetas note, reverse, Spain, 1951. 4 100 lire note, reverse, Italy, 1951.
5 Stamp, 30c, Singapore, 1950s. 6 Chameleon stamp, 9np, Ghana, 1950s. 7 Stamp, USSR, 1958.*

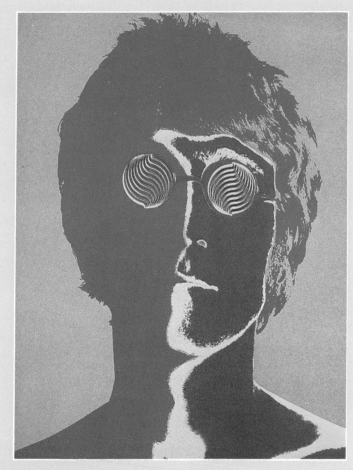

*Psychedelic portrait of John Lennon, Richard Avedon, poster for The Daily Express, Britain, 1967.*

# CHAPTER · FIVE

# 1960
## TO
# 1969

# INTRODUCTION

Youth, prosperity and progress would be the confident themes as America consolidated on the years of peace which followed the Korean War. As a candidate for the presidency of the United States during the 1960 election, John Fitzgerald Kennedy had asked the American people to look about themselves; to look at the nation's schools, shopping centres, highways and above all, their own lives. This has been, he declared, the greatest period of progress in history. Several months later, on 20 January 1961, Kennedy was inaugurated as the thirty-fourth and youngest ever President of the United States of America. His assassination on 22 November 1963 stunned the world.

The passing of the Kennedy years saw an increased military commitment in South Vietnam (an involvement already underway during Kennedy's administration). By 1967 the publicity of prosperity and progress had become joined by the posters of protest. Not only was Vietnam a cause of dissension. The tragic assassination of Martin Luther King in 1968 underlined deep racial problems in American society.

Across the Atlantic, Harold Macmillan had secured a second term as Prime Minister of Great Britain. Continuing national prosperity had been a key factor during the 1959 General Election. 'Life's Better with the Conservatives', proclaimed the hoardings. The public agreed and duly returned the Tories to power with a majority of one hundred parliamentary seats.

In the areas of fashion, pop music and art, Britain assumed world importance after 1962. British 'pop' art took a light-hearted look at American advertising of the previous decade. Famous brandnames now became the subject for 'art', with typical imagery featuring in Derek Boshier's 1962 painting *K's Special*, which depicted a Kellogg's cereal packet and a portrait of cosmonaut Yuri Gagarin – a 'special' symbol of Khrushchev's Russia.

### The United States

Speaking in 1963, Bert Littman, President of the Art Directors Club of New York, stated: 'The Art Directors Club of New York is now the visual communications center of the world. Nowhere else, in any other country, is there such a concentration of activities devoted to the development and presentation of every phase of graphic media.' Littman was probably correct, for New York was where the world looked to for a model on how to handle advertising type, illustration, photography and copywriting. It was not to remain that way after the 1960s.

The creative team of Julian Koenig and Helmut Krone at Doyle Dane Bernbach excelled with their work for Avis automobile rental. Ogilvy considers that Doyle Dane Bernbach '…created one of the most powerful campaigns in the history of advertising'. The headline '*When you're only No.2, you try harder. Or else*' was forthright and reminded its main competitor, Hertz, that in the world of business,

Lemon.

While the motor manufacturing conglomerates of Detroit planned to take a bigger stake overseas, Europe had ambitions on the United States. Smaller cars were euphemistically referred to as 'compact', and most European cars conformed to this definition. The advertising agency Doyle Dane Bernbach continued to devise throughout the decade a series of plain but effective ads for the Volkswagen 'Beetle'. Agency copywriters were, among others, Julian Koenig ('Think small' and 'Lemon'), Janet Boden ('Two can live as cheaply as one'), John Withers ('How to do a Volkswagen ad'), Ron Levin ('Joint savings account'), and John Noble ('Volkswagen build strong bodies 8 ways'). Art directors and graphic designers included Stan Jones, Helmut Krone, Si Lam and Roy Grace. The Volkswagen of America campaign by Doyle Dane Bernbach used outdoor advertising, full-page-space bookings in magazines and television commercials. As David Ogilvy pointed out in his book *Ogilvy on Advertising* (1983), sales of the Beetle went up to 500,000 per year. In a big society as yet unafflicted by economic recession and oil shortages, Dane Doyle Bernbach made small acceptable before Schumacher made it beautiful (the Beetle was hardly elegant in styling).

place ratings are continually changing (a variation of this advertisement was also used by Avis in Britain). A follow-up with copy written by Paula Green, '*Avis is only No.2 in rent-a-cars. So why go with us?*', was equally effective.

The word 'sexism', both as a noun and definition, had yet to be invented. A leading brand of 'king' size cigarettes was advertised as having 'man sized flavor'. Another cigarette, Marlboro, had a mainly female loyalty. Again it was a New York agency, Leo Burnett Company Incorporated, which Philip Morris used in order to devise a campaign to widen its gender appeal. The Marlboro cowboy 'beefed-up' the product image and, more important, its sales as well.

Colour television was part of American life (only one other country, Japan, broadcast in colour in 1960). Black and white television had affected cinema attendances during the 1950s; colour television would increasingly affect newspapers and weekly magazines as the 1960s progressed.

Television presented graphic designers with the problem of how to improve the readability of low resolution, horizontal line formed lettering. The Graphic Arts Department of CBS News designed an alphabet for television news broadcasts. The result was called CBS News 36.

The 1960s would be the swan-song for the American topical magazine. Television could now feature newsreels within hours of an event anywhere in the world. The launching of the world's first communication satellite, *Telstar*, in 1962, allowed live television pictures to be transmitted across the Atlantic for the first time. Across

America, several well-respected daily newspapers folded, and the outlook for magazines was only a little better. After 148 years, publication of *The Saturday Evening Post* ceased and, by the close of the decade, it had been joined by *Look* and *Life*. Although struggling for survival in the face of the television competition, the weekly magazines were remarkable for having a number of talented art editors. For more than fifteen years Allen Hurlburt was art editor of *Look* (he would later live in Britain and become internationally known through his books on graphic design subjects). At *McCall's* the in-house design team was headed by Otto Storch. American 'quality' newspapers underwent a transformation. A new typographic style and page grid was devised for *The New York Times* by its director of design, Louis Silverstein. The Sunday edition of the *New York Herald Tribune* also adopted a new layout scheme, designed by Peter Palazzo.

American corporate design was by now much admired. Eliot Noyes and Paul Rand continued to develop their corporate identity programme for IBM, begun in 1955. Noyes, an industrial designer, was the consultant for much of the IBM product range marketed during the 1960s. Rand designed the IBM logotype, an alphabet and sign system which formed a large part of the IBM *Design Guide*. The Westinghouse visual manifestation programme was also a major corporate project undertaken by Rand. The New York design group of Chermayeff & Geismar Associates was formed in 1960 (formerly Brownjohn, Chermayeff & Geismar). In association with the architectural practice Skidmore, Owings & Merrill, graphic design was undertaken for the Chase Manhattan Bank, Wall Street, New York, sign systems for Libby-Owens-Ford in Toledo, and for United Airlines' terminal at Idlewild Airport, New York. A further link-up took place in 1964, when Ivan Chermayeff and Thomas H. Geismar became two of the founder principals of Cambridge Seven Associates, an architectural and design office in Cambridge, Massachusetts. Cambridge Seven remodelled stations, designed subway cars and signing for the Massachusetts Bay Transportation Authority in Boston in 1965, and exhibition design for the United States Pavilion, at Expo '67. Chermayeff & Geismar's most recognizable mark worldwide was for Mobil in 1966. This replaced the red flying horse symbol with a logotype identificant.

Saul Bass was already known as a designer of film credit titles. Based in Los Angeles, Bass ran a major design office as well, which also carried out much corporate work for, among others, Bell Telephones and United Airlines. Rudolf de Harak had his own New York practice until 1969, when he joined up with Al Corchia to form Corchia de Harak Incorporated. Rudolf de Harak was also a founding principal of Cambridge Seven. He has applied graphic design to interior and exhibition projects. The exhibition scheme for the Man and his World pavilion at Expo '67 was carried out by de Harak for the Canadian Government. Rudolf de Harak

taught during this period at The Cooper Union School of Art and Architecture, New York.

There follows brief biographies of key graphic designers of the period. First, Louis Danziger, who specialized in advertising design and packaging. In 1964 he joined the staff of the Chouinard Art School (later to become the California Institute of the Arts), Los Angeles.

Herb Lubalin (1918–1981) had a preoccupation with the assembly of letters to form decorative logotypes. A hallmark of his work was often a 'baroque' swirling ampersand. Good examples of Lubalin magazine logotypes were for *Mother & Child* (1966) and *The Saturday Evening Post* (1968).

Milton Glaser was synonymous throughout the 1960s for his association with the Push Pin Studios (founded by Glaser, Seymour Chast and Ed Sorel in 1954). Bright colours and full letterforms were characteristics of his work at this time.

## Britain

Cigarette advertising featured prominently in newspapers, magazines and on television during the early 1960s. The 1957 report of the Medical Research Council informed British smokers about the link between smoking and lung cancer. The tobacco companies sought to preserve their sales by the introduction of new brands and new psychological packaging strategies. The first of the brands marketed in response to the lung cancer scare was Guards, which was launched in 1958. A filter cigarette, it featured a pack with a white background field. Guards made filter cigarettes acceptable to men and its packaging relied on ancient associations of white and purity. Advertised on television, Guards was to remain a brand leader throughout the 1960s. Other makes soon followed suit and, by 1962, many brands had adopted the white background formula. Player's Medium 'Navy Cut' lost its famous 'seascape' pack and the floral extravagancy of Will's 'Wild Woodbine' had been pruned into simple rectangles.

Britain's fast-growing independent commercial television companies were able to attract young talents in the field of graphic design, many of whom had studied at the Royal College of Art. Perhaps the most notable company was ABC Television Limited, which had its production facility at Teddington, on the Western outskirts of London. ABC was a subsidiary of the Associated British Picture Corporation, a name famous as a British cinema circuit. June Fraser of the Design Research Unit designed their motif, which created a separate personality for the television operation of the ABC group. This was perhaps the most striking company call sign on British television until ABC lost their broadcasting franchise in 1968.

The popularity of television as a conveyor of current affairs and actuality had been achieved at the expense of the printed word. It was time for change in the newspaper

*Conservative Party election poster, Britain, 1959.*

# INTRODUCTION

industry. Well-respected nationals such as *The News Chronicle* and *The Daily Herald* would disappear during the decade. In 1962 *The Sunday Times* introduced its colour supplement, which would transform the lifestyle of a young, largely university educated readership. Four years later *The Times* at last put news on its front page. New technology also began to spell the end of traditional printing methods, as a quiet revolution took place in the provinces when larger local newspapers became printed by web offset (printing by offset lithography on a continuous length of paper or web).

For many British families, motoring finally became a reality. The Ministry of Transport embarked on a thousand mile motorway construction programme. Higher traffic speeds required modern road signs. Starting in 1959, Jock Kinneir devised an alphabet, bifurcation devices and service area pictogrammes for use on motorways. The report of the Worboys' Committee in 1963, which looked at the need to provide traffic signs for general purpose roads, recommended the adoption of a modified scheme based on the pattern formulated by the 1949 United Nations conference on road signs. Once again, Jock Kinneir developed his motorway alphabet, now called Transport, and designed a comprehensive set of pictogrammes. Substantial regard was also given to the environmental suitability of the new 'continental' signs.

The consecration of Coventry Cathedral in 1962 symbolized the completion of the nation's post-war recovery. Bomb sites were gone and in their place in towns like Plymouth, Portsmouth, Coventry, Liverpool and Southampton stood new department stores, multiples and supermarkets. Graphic designers would be kept busy creating new house styles, packaging ranges, store sign systems and ticketing layouts. Typical of these nationwide combines is J. Sainsbury Limited (which had a much admired in-house design studio under Peter Dixon). But behind this high street bustle was a scene of urban renewal as the demolition contractors cleared away slums and sometimes, much to the horror of the public, historic buildings.

In spite of many brash new buildings, there were still exceptions. The estate for Span, designed by Eric Lyons at Blackheath Park, London (completed 1962) and the homes built by Wates at Coulsdon, Surrey (1967), would provide archetypes for middle-class housing. The building and construction boom also saw a visual manifestation in the way that the more progressive companies applied graphic design for the first time. Foremost were Wates and Taylor Woodrow. In both cases F.H.K. Henrion was asked to give them new trademarks and an accompanying corporate image. Wates, a well-known firm which had built acres of housing estates in the London area, now replaced their dark green vehicle and grey plant livery for a bright yellow scheme.

A nationwide look at the visual appearance of the railways

*British Rail signs, Design Research Unit, Britain, c.1965.*

was to occur in 1964, when the Design Research Unit was commissioned to create a new corporate identity programme. Unveiled on 1 January 1965, it had a new geometric 'rail' symbol by Gerald Barney, together with an alphabet for signing, printed display and use on rolling stock by Jock Kinneir. In addition, new housecolours and the shortened name of 'British Rail' were adopted.

Gas had a similar problem to the railways in so far as it had a nineteenth century association. If steam trains were slow and dirty, gasworks gave off an unpleasant smell and the resulting coal gas was not considered to be a clean fuel by the consumer. The industry had been taken into state ownership in 1947. The various gas boards used the 'Mr Therm' trademark. This reminded the British public of the Second World War when government information material had featured the famous 'Squander Bug', a creature who by creating waste aided the enemy. The image of gas smacked of government control and memories of austerity during the 1940s and 1950s.

A brilliant advertising campaign in 1966 put the headline *High Speed Gas* across the hoardings. The copywriting owed much to contemporary petrol advertising. It was the era of 'Getaway People Get Super National' (National Benzole), 'Get Out of Town Fast' (Regent) and 'Put a Tiger in Your Tank' (Esso). If white worked for cigarettes, it would also imply cleanliness when used on showroom fascia panels and fleet vehicles. Mr Therm was dead and in his place now stood crisp blue Helvetica lettering on a white field. The legend simply said 'Gas'. The campaign and its associated corporate identity programme halted the slide of customers to electricity. The new energy source of natural gas was about to be discovered in the North Sea. With the 'flame from the sea' gasworks would vanish and become part of British industrial mythology.

The 1960s were a time for visual change in the public sector. In 1965 local government reform set up the Greater London Council (GLC), and with it new enlarged London boroughs. As many of these included a collection of rival old established towns, new generic borough names had to be created in some places. Graphic design was a key ingredient in endowing boroughs with a corporate being. Notable work was done by Main Wolff & Partners for the London Borough of Camden.

Government departments began to disseminate clearer public information. Forms, booklets and leaflets now showed the hand of trained graphic designers. At Her Majesty's Stationery Office (HMSO), John Westwood and Peter Branfield set new standards. The General Post Office (GPO) was a government department which had a tradition of public relations extending back to the 1930s. By the early 1960s the philatelic trade was successful in making the GPO bring out brighter stamps. The return of the Labour Party to power, in 1964, resulted in Anthony Wedgwood Benn being appointed Postmaster-General. This proved a favourable step forward and Wedgwood Benn soon stimulated an enlightened period of design awareness within the Post Office (as it became in 1968). In 1968 Stuart Rose became the Design Adviser to the Post Office. The growing importance of stamp design as an art college area of study was shown in the appointment of Andrew Restall as first Fellow in Stamp Design at the Royal College of Art in 1969.

Publishing was another example of British excellence during the 1960s. Penguin Books attracted national attention when an Old Bailey court case allowed them to publish D. H. Lawrence's controversial book *Lady Chatterley's Lover* in 1960, but the real revolution for the publishing house was not sexual but visual. With the Italian designer Germano Facetti as Art Director, Penguin strengthened their housestyle and employed a standard cover grid devised by Romek Marber. Consultant art editor at Thames and Hudson was George Adams, who designed their 'World of Art' series. Another publisher with a distinctive housestyle was Studio Vista. Their series of topical books about design, architecture and film under the editorship of John Lewis provided valuable information for design professionals and students alike. Titles in this series included *Basic Design* by Maurice de Saumarez, *Typography* by John Lewis, *Graphic Design, Visual Comparisons* by Alan Fletcher, Colin Forbes and Bob Gill, *Trademarks* by Peter Wildbur and *Graphics Handbook* by Ken Garland.

### France

Although France had a proud fine art reputation, it had also made an important contribution to typefounding in previous centuries, a tradition continued by Deberny & Peignot. A popular typeface was Antique Olive, designed in 1962 by Roger Excoffon (1910-1983).

A new generation of graphic artists was represented by the posters of Raymond Savignac, André François and Bernard Villemot.

An illustrator whose work acquired an international reputation was André François. In the true French manner, François studied at the École des Beaux-Arts and then in the Ecole A. M. Cassandre. His illustrations appeared in *Vogue*, *The New Yorker* and *Punch*. In addition, his posters and press advertisements made his name well-known to a wide public.

Events in Paris during May 1968, when there were angry street disturbances and riots, brought a flood of crude but powerful posters on to the city walls.

### Germany

In the Federal Republic the Ulm and Basle colleges became the most influential art schools since the Bauhaus. The Bauhaus had been closed by the Nazis and the Ulm college was opened in 1949 by the 'Scholl Foundation' in order to perpetuate the memory of the 'White Rose',

*'The Process' by Kafka, Roman Cieslewicz, France, 1964.*

a group of Munich students who resisted the Nazi régime at the cost of their own lives in 1943. Both Anthony Froshaug (1920-1984) and Stankowski taught at Ulm. In 1962 Otl Aicher was appointed its Vice-Chancellor. Students there included Peter von Kornatzki, Frank Memelsdorf (who is now a partner in the Barcelona design group Rolando & Memelsdorf) and Rolf Müller.

Leipzig had been the centre of German book production prior to the Second World War, and already by the late 1940s the Hochschule für Graphik und Buchkunst (College for Graphic and Book Art) in Leipzig had re-opened. Book design and illustration had remained an important part of graphic design in the GDR.

Other colleges of art came back into being in Dresden and East Berlin. At the Kunsthochschule (College of Art) in East Berlin, the Professor for Graphic Design since 1956 has been Werner Klemke. Klemke is one of the GDR's best illustrators, who engraves on wood. He is an acknowledged expert on the typography of Jan Tschichold and has written the introduction to several publications about him, including a re-print of Tschichold's 1925 essay *Elementare Typographie*.

The best-known graphic designers were Anton Stankowski and Willy Fleckhaus. Stankowski's approach was formal and structured. In 1965 he was asked to create a new graphic housestyle for West Berlin. The result was *Das Berlin-Layout*. Fleckhaus was renowned for his 'twelve-unit' layout grid for the magazine *Twen*. In addition, he designed many of its covers.

Other graphic designers to emerge in the GDR during the 1960s were Gert Wunderlich (a poster artist with a strong interest in typeface design), Rudolf Grüttner (a poster artist who is also a Professor at the College of Art in East Berlin) and Otto Kummert, who became head of the artists' workshop at Progress Film Distributors and has also designed trademarks, book jackets and television titles.

*Pirelli magazine advertisement, Andre Francois, France, 1963.*

### Canada

In 1867 the British Parliament had granted Canada a large measure of autonomy, but it was not until 1965 that Canada's own national flag was approved. Featuring a strong red maple leaf device, it soon formed the basis for graphic design applications. The senior designer at Stewart & Morrison was Hans Kleefeld. Another leading design group was Design Collaborative, founded by Rolf Harder and Ernst Roch. Their poster for the Design Canada section at the XIV Milan Triennale in 1968, again made principal use of a repeat arrangement of red maple leaves.

Canada was one of the first countries to develop a national visual identity programme. Canadian design was presented to a home and (as already mentioned, with participation at Milan), an overseas public. The 'Design

# INTRODUCTION

Canada' visual image adopted by the National Design Council was notable and, by 1970, an 'Information Canada Office' had been formed. The Federal Identity Programme team, known as 'FIP Team', started to co-ordinate all government graphic design. A bi-lingual official requirement has resulted in high standards of architectural signing, information design and printed matter produced by FIP Team.

## Italy

The Italian companies Pirelli and Olivetti were known for outstanding design. As they both had worldwide operations, it was understandable that many non-Italian designers would work for them.

In 1964 Pirelli issued their first calendar, designed by Derek Birdsall. This, and subsequent calendars, would be eagerly sought after and became collectors' items. Pirelli's advertising was memorable for the London bus side poster designed by Fletcher/Forbes/Gill and an amusing variation of the Pirelli logotype by André François. The Italian parent company had publicity designed for them by Bob Noorda, Martin Engelmann, Albe Steiner and the Studio Boggeri.

Olivetti had used Herbert Bayer, Paul Rand and Savignac to design advertisements in the years after the Second World War, and during the early 1960s Walter Ballmer and Max Huber, together with Giovanni Pintori, would continue to create much of the Milan-produced Olivetti advertising.

In publishing, the firm of A. Mondadori, under its art director Anita Klinz, developed a strikingly simple but effective housestyle. Many of their books were notable for having covers designed by the abstract painters Capogrossi, Baj, Lucio Fontana and Scanavino.

Private press work centred on German-born Giovanni Mardesteig and his Officina Bondoni in Verona. Mardersteig was also known for his typeface designs.

---

**HELVE UNIVEF**

Basle had been an early centre of type founding during the sixteenth century. The Haas foundry cut its Neues Haas Grotesk typeface. Designed by Max Miedinger in 1958, it would become widely available and later known as Helvetica. The other dominant typeface of the 1960s was Univers, designed by Adrian Frutiger, who was appointed art director of the Paris typefounders, Deberny & Peignot in 1958. Conceived as a *universal* fount, Univers was one of the first typefaces to be created for filmsetting, in addition for hot-metal use. The two veterans of European type designing, Hungarian-born Imre Reiner and Jan Tschichold, both continued working in Switzerland. Tschichold's typeface Sabon appeared in 1967.

---

Several Italian graphic designers spent a period of time working overseas. Massimo Vignelli went to New York and Germano Facetti became art editor at Penguin Books in Britain.

## Switzerland

As a small neutral state in the middle of Europe, Switzerland had been unique in being able to preserve an aesthetic continuity throughout the decades leading up to the 1960s. The reputation of Swiss graphic design in the 1960s was to spread throughout Europe, North America and Japan. As in the 1930s, activity was primarily based on Basle and Zurich, although Berne would also be known for high-quality graphic design. The Zurich pioneers, Max Bill, Hans Neuburg, Richard P. Lohse and Josef Müller-Brockmann were international figures in graphic design. There follows a brief biography of each of these key figures.

Max Bill was Rector of Ulm College of Design, 1951/56. He would be active in Swiss politics until 1967, when he was appointed Professor at the Staatliche Hochschule für Bildende Künste (State College of Fine Arts) in Hamburg.

Following on from the Zurich pioneers came Emil Ruder (1914-1970). He completed a compositor's apprenticeship, finally studying at the Zurich School of Art and Crafts between 1941/42. Ruder would become influential as a teacher at the Basle School of Art and Crafts. His articles in the magazine *Typographische Monatsblätter*, and his book, *Typographie* (later published in the English-speaking world as *Typography*), 1962, would become seminal writings to a generation of typographers being educated in Europe and the United States during the late 1960s. He was, arguably, along with Müller-Brockmann and Armin Hofmann, the greatest typographic force since Tschichold.

Continuing the Swiss tradition of the graphic designer/fine artist was Karl Gerstner. His paintings were formed on a rational structure and work in the graphic design discipline has followed a similiar pattern of aesthetic thought. His layout grid for the Swiss magazine *Capital* was one of the

---

Graphic design became an international profession during the 1960s, and events such as Olympiads were prestige occasions for the host nations. In 1964 Tokyo Olympics used pictogram information devices for the first time on a large scale. The Olympic graphic programme was directed by Masura Katzumie. The Olympic symbol was devised by Yusaka Kamekura, who also created a number of posters incorporating the photography of Osamu Hayasaki with typography. At the 1968 Olympiad held in Mexico, an international team of designers helped co-ordinate all the public information design. The graphic director was Lance Wyman from New York, working with the London design group Peter Murdoch Partnership and Eduardo Terrazas. A distinctive logotype and associated pictogram system was part of a number of elements created for the Games.

*Tokyo Olympics pictogram, Masura Katzumie, Japan, 1964.*

Armin Hofmann studied in Zurich and, after a lithographic apprenticeship in Winterthur, joined the teaching staff of Basle School of Art and Crafts in 1947. Hofmann became internationally-known, particularly in the United States, from the mid-1950s onwards. He taught at Philadelphia School of Art and was a guest lecturer at Yale University. As is the case with much Swiss graphic design output; museums, art galleries, regional authorities and fairs have provided projects. During the late 1950s and 1960s Hofmann designed posters for cultural events (among other work). In 1964 he designed the monogram 'E' and Swiss flag device for the Schweizerische Landesausstellung (Swiss National Expo '64 at Lausanne, held twenty-five years after the 1939 Zurich LA). Armin Hofmann has also become known through his book *Graphic Design Manual*.

most ingenious ever devised. The growth of computer technology during the 1960s found Gerstner examining the possibilities of creating visual schemes. The result was published as a book, *Designing Programmes* (1964).

Carlo L. Vivarelli was co-editor of *Neue Grafik*. He studied with the Paris poster artist Paul Colin (as had F. H. K. Henrion before him). After a short period in 1946 as art director for Studio Boggeri in Milan, he returned to his native Zurich. In 1958 he showed some of his designs along with Neuburg and Lohse at the *Konstuktive Grafik* (Constructive Graphic Art) exhibition at the Zurich Kunstgewerbemuseum.

In 1965 the Zurich design office of Odermatt and Tissi was founded by Siegfried Odermatt and Rosmarie Tissi. Siegfried Odermatt was largely self-taught and had practised as a freelance graphic designer since 1950. Rosmarie Tissi studied at the Zurich School of Arts and Crafts. Their work during the 1960s included press advertising and brochures for the computer company, Sperry Rand Univac.

## The Netherlands

In January 1963, the founding of Total Design established The Netherlands' 'eerste combinatiebureau' – the 'first combined discipline office' or design group. The founders were the graphic designers Wim Crouwel and Benno Wissing (also an architectural designer), the industrial designer Friso Kramer, together with Dick and Paul Schwarz, who handled the accounting and management side of the group. A further graphic designer, Ben Bos, joined Total soon afterwards.

Major Total Design projects in the 1960s were the sign system for Amsterdam Schipol Airport, catalogues for the Stedelijk Museum and a corporate identity programme for PAM petrol, a part of the mineral company Steenkolen Handelsvereenging NV. In 1967 Wim Crouwel designed a set of letterforms for digital generation by computers. Called 'New Alphabet', each character had an equal width (one unit). In 1968 Helmut Kowalke joined Total, by which time the group had grown to twenty-one members. Just over a year later a figure of forty people would be reached.

# PACKAGING

*1 & 2* IBM office material, Paul Rand, US, 1960s. *3* Omo detergent pack, Britain, 1960s. *4* Food and household goods, Britain, 1960s. *5* Sunsip shandy, Britain, 1960s.

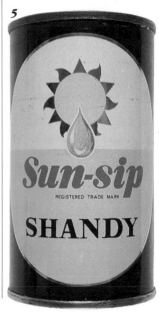

120

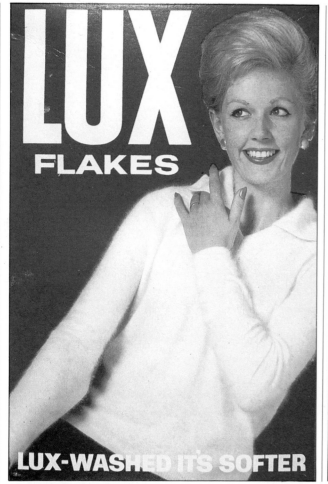

LUX FLAKES

LUX-WASHED IT'S SOFTER

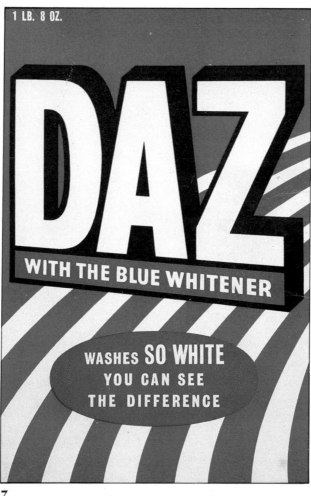

1 LB. 8 OZ.

DAZ

WITH THE BLUE WHITENER

WASHES **SO WHITE** YOU CAN SEE THE DIFFERENCE

ROBIN Starch

**8**

**6** Lux flakes packaging, Lever Brothers Ltd, Britain, 1965.
**7** Daz soap powder packaging, Proctor & Gamble Ltd, Britain, 1965. **8** Robin starch packaging, Reckitt & Sons Ltd, Britain, 1965.

BIRDS EYE

2 Beefburgers

**12**

**6**

**9**

**7**

**NEWS!**
Add 3 tablespoons to your Weekly Wash for Extra Cleaning Power

Flash

Once-over cleaner for LINOLEUM, FLOORS, WALLS, PAINTWORK

NO RINSING! NO WIPING DRY!

**11**

**TRIAL OFFER**

Crest **6**<sup>D</sup>.

TOOTH PASTE

OFF

**10**

Freece Tooth Paste *with* P S Boots

**9** Flash soap powder packaging, Thomas Hedley & Co., Britain, 1965. **10** Crest toothpaste packaging, Proctor & Gamble Ltd, Britain, 1964. **11** Freece toothpaste packaging, Boots Ltd, Britain, 1964. **12** Birds Eye beefburgers packaging, Britain, 1964.

*Moment of pleasure*

KENT
CIGARETTES
NEW
EXCLUSIVE MICRONITE FILTER

KING SIZE

KING SIZE
KENT®

First with the finest cigarettes through Lorillard Research

Kent with the MICRONITE filter gives you the best combination of filter-action and satisfying taste

© 1964 P. Lorillard Co.

When you've time to enjoy a moment of pleasure—try Kent. You get the good taste of Kent's "Flavor-Matured" tobaccos filtered through the famous "Micronite" filter.

FOR THE BEST COMBINATION OF FILTER AND GOOD TASTE **KENT** satisfies best

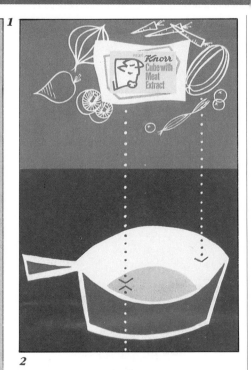

1

Knorr Cube with Meat Extract

2

3

4

shop
at
Ohrbach's
MENS SHOP

34TH STREET OPPOSITE EMPIRE STATE BUILDING · OPEN MONDAYS AND THURSDAY NIGHTS TILL 9

5

If you have a problem in Foreign Exchange talk to the people at Chase Manhattan

One man especially qualified to help you is Vice President William H. Lantz.

Head of Foreign Exchange Trading for the Bank's International Department, Bill Lantz has been a Chaseman for 32 years with 29 years devoted entirely to Foreign Exchange Trading.

During this time he has toured the money markets of the free world many times over and maintained an active role in international exchange organizations.

Bill Lantz' long practical experience plus his many close personal contacts with exchange specialists abroad make him a valuable man to know if you have a foreign exchange problem.

You can reach him by writing to 1 Chase Manhattan Plaza, New York 15, N.Y.

THE CHASE MANHATTAN BANK

Member Federal Deposit Insurance Corporation

6

1 *Kent cigarette advertisement, US, 1964.* 2 *Knorr food advertisement from Woman magazine, Britain, 1960.* 3 *Pirelli advertisement, Bob Noorda, Italy, early 1960s.* 4 *Olivetti advertisement, Giovanni Pintori, Italy, 1960.* 5 *Ohrbach's (men's shop) advertisement, Doyle Dane Bernbach advertising agency, US, 1960s.* 6 *Chase Manhattan Bank advertisement, US, 1962.* 7 *Volkswagen advertisement, Doyle Dane Bernbach advertising agency, US, 1969.* 8 *AC spark plugs advertisement, US, 1963.*

Ugly is only skin-deep.

7

AC Spark Plugs give you full gasoline power

Today's gasolines are refined to give top mileage, peak power. Ideal mates for AC Fire-Ring Spark Plugs because ...

ACs unleash maximum gasoline power with a full-bodied spark; give full power longer because they're self-cleaning.

AC's exclusive Hot Tip design heats faster to burn off power-robbing deposits ... puts the big punch in your gasoline.

To get all the power you pay for at the pump—team up your favorite gasoline with new AC Fire-Ring Spark Plugs.

AC FIRE-RING SPARK PLUGS

8

# POSTERS

**End Bad Breath.**

**1** *'End Bad Breath', Seymour Chwast, US, 1969-70.* **2** *Film poster, Nico, Cuba, 1969.* **3** *Bob Dylan, Milton Glaser, US.* **4** *'The Different Drummer', Peter Max, US, 1968.* **5** *Poster for the Tokyo 1964 Olympic Games, Yasaku Kamekura, Japan, 1964.*

4

5

# POSTERS

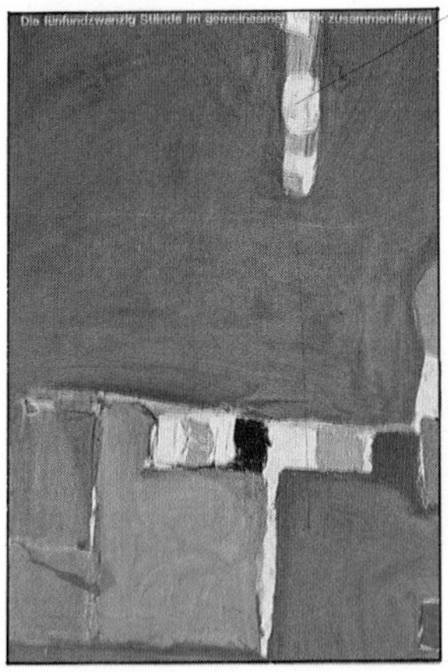

1

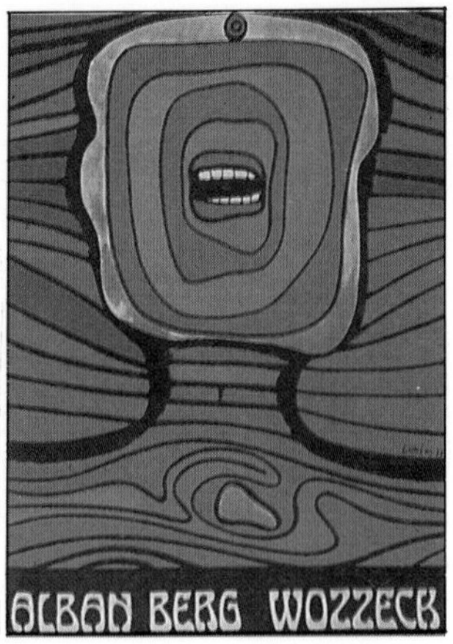
ALBAN BERG WOZZECK

2

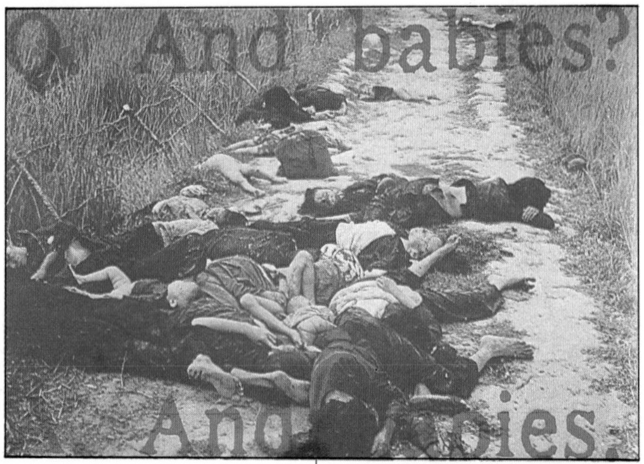
Q. And babies?

3

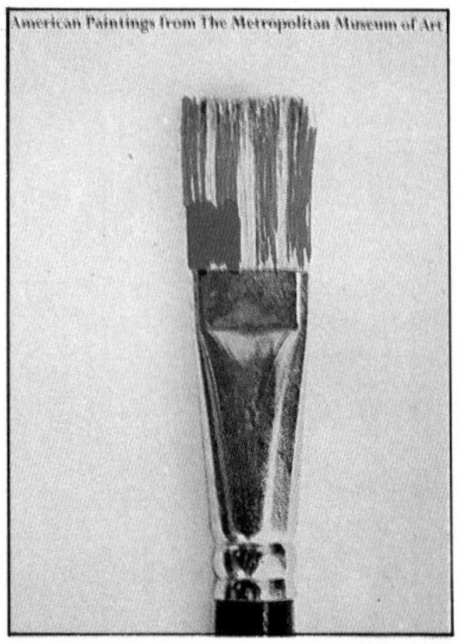
American Paintings from The Metropolitan Museum of Art

4

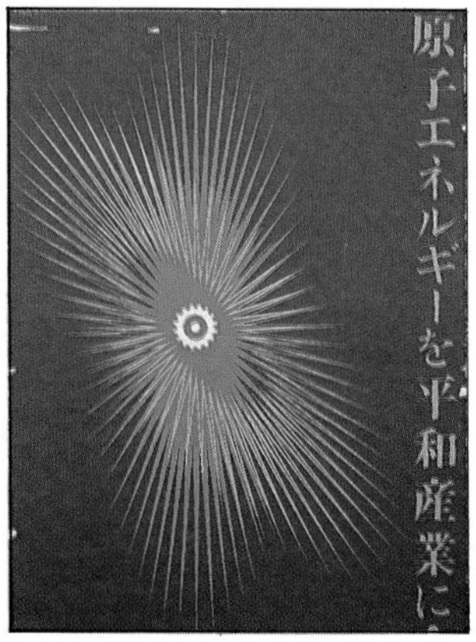
原子エネルギーを平和産業に

5

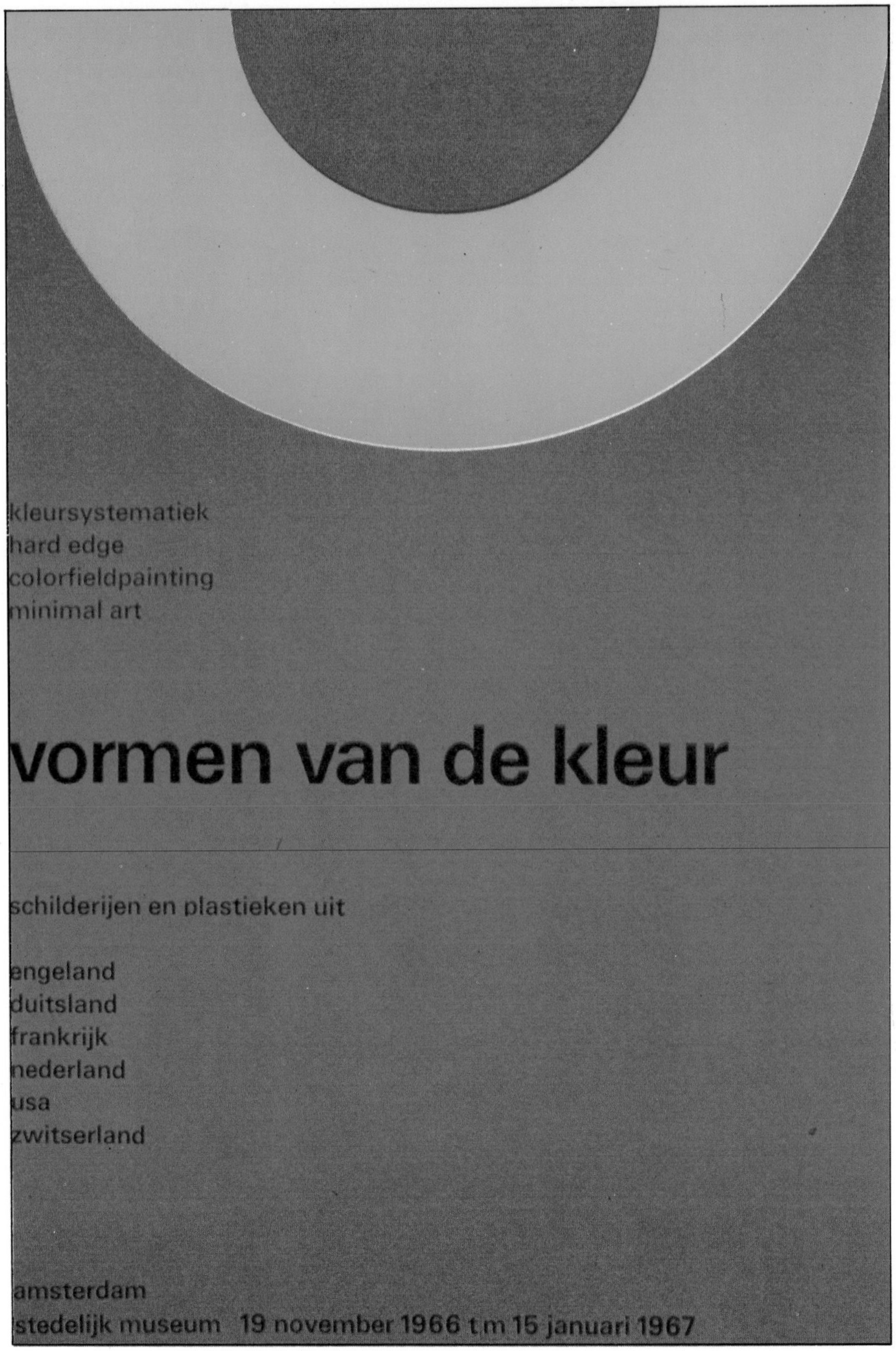
kleursystematiek
hard edge
colorfieldpainting
minimal art
vormen van de kleur
schilderijen en plastieken uit
engeland
duitsland
frankrijk
nederland
usa
zwitserland
amsterdam
stedelijk museum 19 november 1966 t/m 15 januari 1967

6

*1 '25 Exhibition Stands ...', Hans Falk, Switzerland, 1964. 2 Poster for the opera 'Wozzeck' by Alban Berg, Jan Lenica, Poland, 1964. 3 'Q. And babies? A. And babies', Peter Brandt with photography by R.L.Haeberle, US, 1970. 4 Poster for 'American Painting from the Metropolitan Museum of Art', Louis Danziger, US, 1966. 5 Atoms for Peace, Yasaku Kamekura, Japan, 1965. 6 'Forms of Colour', Wim Crouwel, Netherlands, 1967.*

# MAGAZINES

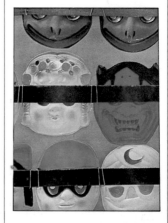

**1** OZ, cover by Peter Brookes, Australia, c.1969. **2 & 3** Look, art editor Allen Hurlburt, US, January 1961 and September 1963. **4** Look, feature spread using Will Hopkins' 'Twelve-unit' grid, photography by Art Kane, US, September 1963. **5** OZ, cover by Joshua Thomas, British publication, c.1969. **6** Teen Time, US, September 1962.

# MAGAZINES

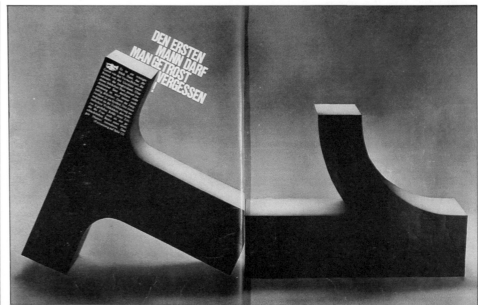

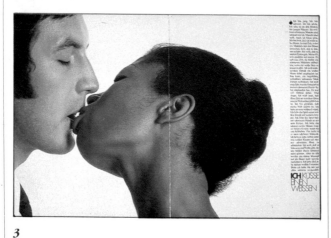

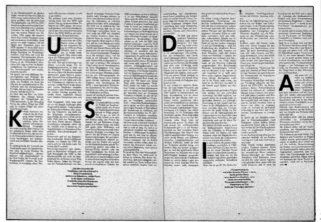

**1** *Twen visuals by Willy Fleckhaus, W.Germany, July 1969.* **2** *Double page spread from Twen. 3 Spread from Twen, January 1969.* **4** *Spread from Twen, July 1969.* **5** *Spread from Twen, January 1969.* **6** *Archigram No 6, cover by Geoff Reeve, Britain, 1965.*

# MAGAZINES

THE SUNDAY TIMES *magazine*

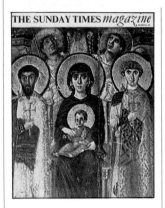

**1**

## Living On Ice
### by Alan Moorehead

It is twice as big as Europe, yet until recently no one lived there but seals and penguins. Now there is a nightly film show at McMurdo Sound, where explorers and scientists are paving the way for life on the moon. Here Alan Moorehead, the traveller and author, reports on his visit earlier this year to the world of Antarctica

**2**

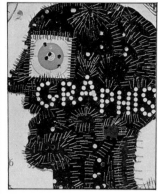

**3**

**NOVA**

50 YEARS AFTER THE VOTE: ONLY THE CHAINS HAVE CHANGED

**4**

## The best threepenny-worth in London
by John Gale. Photographs by Colin Jones

**5**

*international times*
april 28 may 12 · 1/-

**6**

*1 The Sunday Times magazine,
Britain, December 1964.
2 Spread from the Sunday
Times magazine, December
1964. 3 Graphis 106, cover by
André François, Switzerland,
1963. 4 Nova, art editor
David Hillman, Britain, 1968.
5 Feature spread from Nova,
Britain, August 1969.
6 International Times, Britain,
c.1969-70.*

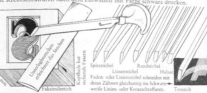

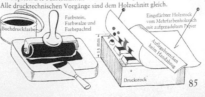

*1* 'Über das Buch' by Heinrich Hussmann, Guido Pressler Verlag, Germany, 1968. *2* Title page from 'Über das Buch', 1968. **3 & 4** Spreads from 'Über das Buch', 1968.

# BOOKS

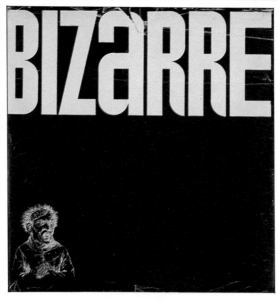

1

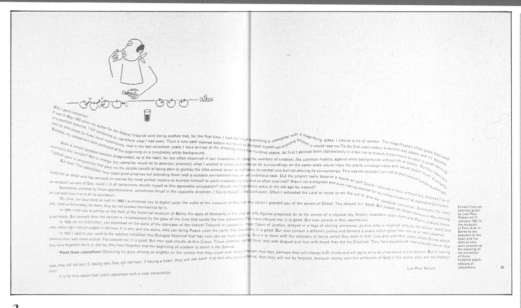

2

3

4

5

1 'Bizarre' by Barrie
Humphries, Elek Brooks,
Britain, 1965. 2 Spread from
'Bizarre', 1965. 3 Spread from
'The Complete Home Guide to

Gardening and Cooking', Paul
Hamlyn Books, Britain, 1963.
4 & 5 Spreads from 'A Time of
Gods', art director George
Adams, Britain, c.1960.

6

7

8

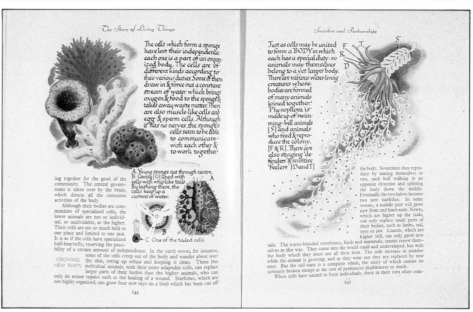

9

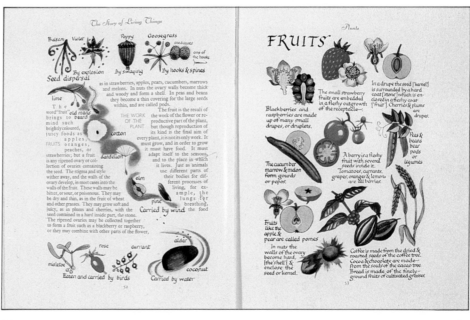

10

6 'The Old Man and the Sea' by Ernest Hemingway, Jonathan Cape, Britain, 1969. 7 'Scandal '63: The Profumo Sensation' by Clive Irving, Ron Hall and Jeremy Wallington, Mayflower Books, Britain, 1961. 8 Back cover of 'The Deep' by Mickey Spillane, Corgi Books, Britain, 1961. 9 & 10 Spread from 'The Story of Living Things and the Evolution', by Eileen Mayo, Waverly Book Company, Britain, 1960s.

# RECORD SLEEVES

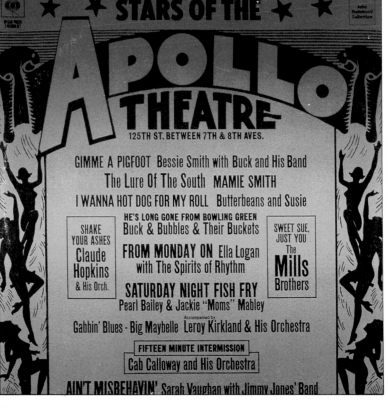

1 'Friends', The Beach Boys, EMI Records, Britain, 1968. 2 'From Hank, Bruce, Brian and John', The Shadows, EMI Records, Britain, 1967. 3 'Disraeli Gears', Cream, illustrator Martin Sharp and photographer Bob Whittaker, Britain, 1967. 4 'Stars of the Apollo Theatre', CBS Records, US, 1973.

5

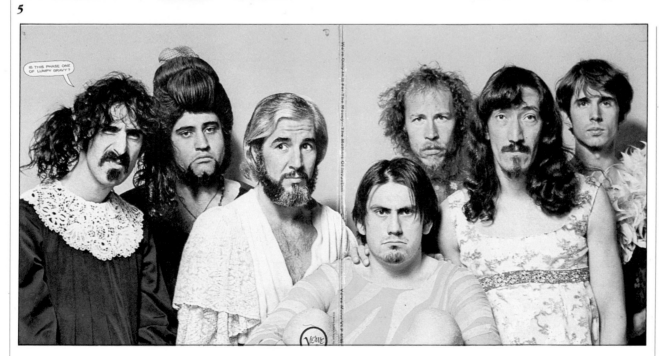

6

**5** *'We're only in it for the money', Frank Zappa and The Mothers, Veuve Records, US, 1968.* **6** *Inside cover of 'We're only in it for the money', 1968.*

# SYMBOLS AND TRADEMARKS

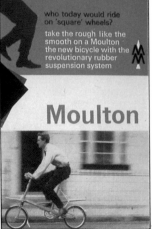

**1** *Mobil Graphic Standards Manual, Eliot Noyes, US, 1966.*
**2** *Wates corporate identity, F.H.K.Henrion, Britain, 1960.*

**3** *KLM Dutch airlines corporate identity, F.H.K.Henrion, Britain, c.1964.* **4** *Moulton Bicycles identity scheme, Banks*
*& Miles, Britain, 1963.* **5** *BEA corporate Identity, F.H.K.Henrion, Britain, c.1968.*

**10**

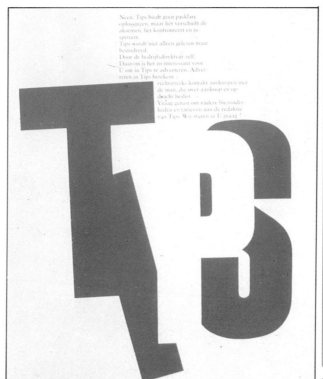

**6** *Berlin-Layout corporate identity, Anton Stankowski for Land Berlin, W.Germany, 1965 onwards.*
**7** *Westinghouse logo, Paul Rand, US, 1960.* **8** *The Magnificent Seven 'trademark', Saul Bass, US, 1960.* **9** *TIPS logo, Rosmarie Tissi, Switzerland, 1968.*
**10** *Information booth, Mexican Olympic Games, 1968.*

6

7

8

9

# INFORMATION DESIGN

1 *Diagram showing division of oceans and continents on the earth's surface, World Atlas, Büchergilde Gutenberg, Germany, 1963.* 2 *Diagram of a fold mountain, World Atlas, Büchergilde Gutenberg, Germany, 1963.* 3 *Diagram showing foreign tourist traffic into Austria, World Atlas, Büchergilde Gutenberg, Germany, 1963.*

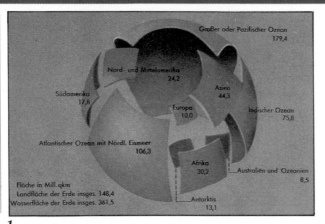

1

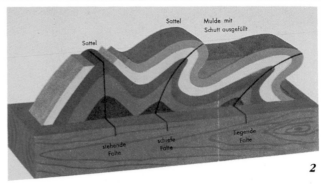

2

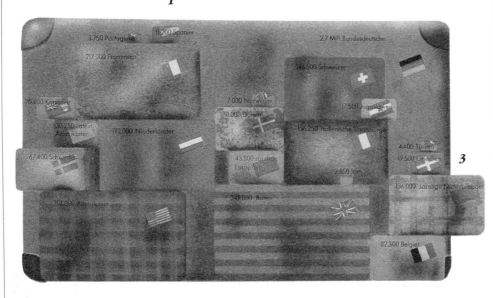

3

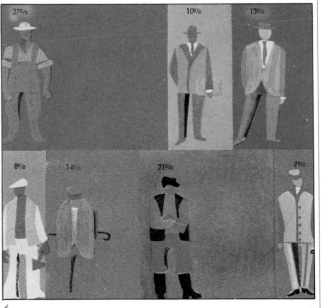

4

4 *Diagram showing cross-section of professions in Denmark, World Atlas, Büchergilde Gutenberg, Germany, 1963.*
5 *Road signs and directions, Britain, 1960.*

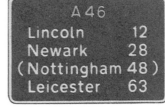

5

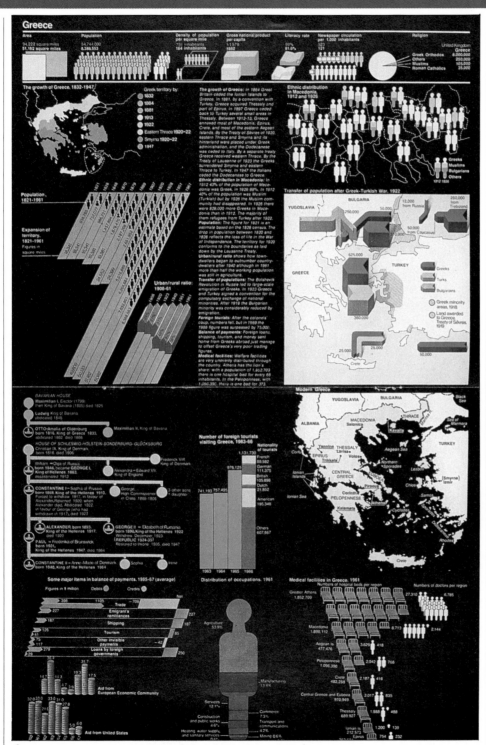

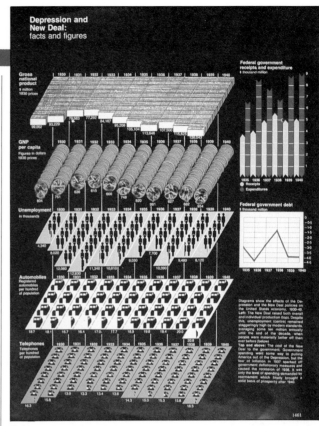

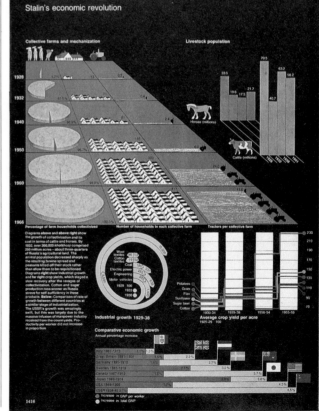

6 Centre spread from 'The History of the 20th Century', illustrated by Diagram, Britain. 7 & 8 Pages from 'The History of the 20th Century'.

# TYPOGRAPHY

A B C D E F G H I J K L M N O P Q R S T U V W X Y Z  Ä Ö Ü  Æ OE

a b c d e f g h i j k l m n o p q r s t u v w x y z

§& 1234567890 ß

**1** Eras, Studio Hollenstein, Wagner, France, 1969.

ABCDEFGHIJKLMMNOPQRSTUVWXYZ
abcdefghijklmnopqrstuvwxyz
1234567890

**2** Syntax, Hand Eduard Meyer, Stempel, 1969.

ABCDEFGHIJKLMNOPQRSTUVXYZW
abcdefghijklmnopqrstuvxyzw
1234567890

**3** Eurostile, A.Novarese, Nebiolo, Italy, 1962.

**ABCDEEFGHIJKLMNNOOPQRRSSTTWXYZ**
**aabccdeeffgghijkllmmnoopqrrssttuvwxyz**
**12345678900**

**4** Adlib, Freeman Craw, American Typefounders, US, 1961.

**ABCDEFGHIJKLMNOPQRSTUVWXYZ**
**abcdefghijklmnopqrstuvwxyz** **1234567890**

**5** Compacta, Letraset, Britain, 1963.

# BANK NOTES AND STAMPS

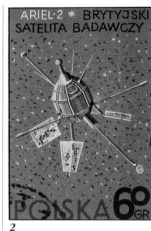

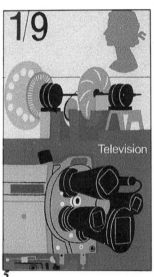

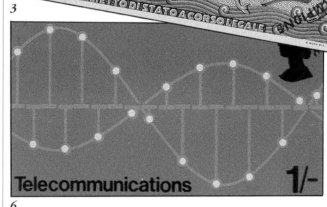

**1** USA air mail stamp, 21c, 1960s. **2** Ariel 2, T.Michaluk, Poland, 1966. **3** 500 lire note, R.Mura, Italy, c.1965. **4** Tunisian stamps, 1960s. **5** Television stamp, 1/9, William Sharland, Britain, 1960s. **6** British Post Office Technology issue, David Gentleman, Britain, 1969. **7** Salvation Army centenary 3d stamp, Britain, 1965.

**8** Salvation Army centenary 1/6 stamp, Britain, 1965. **9** Thai stamp, 1968. **10** Czechoslovakian stamp, J.Lukavsky, 1967.

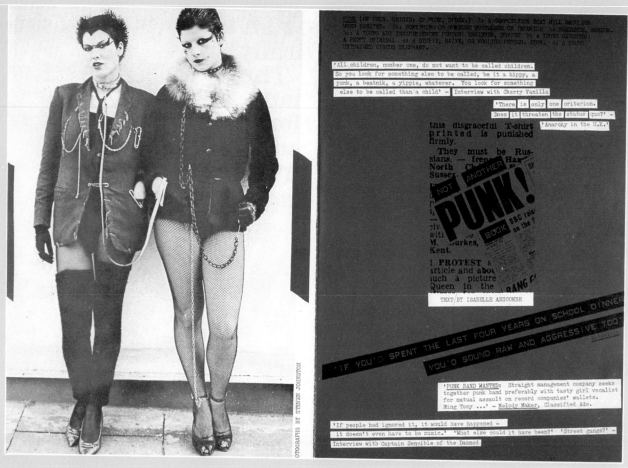

*Spread from 'Not Another Punk Book', Britain, c.1979.*

# CHAPTER · SIX

# 1970
## —TO—
# 1979

# INTRODUCTION

After the affluence and rebellion of the 1960s, the 1970s were largely characterized by economic instability and soul-searching. The world oil crisis of 1973/74 and other shortages, such as paper in England, brought on the great mood of Social Conscience. People generally became more aware and more critical of their own health, diet and lifestyle. Globally there was growing concern for the environment and vanishing resources, the rights of special needs groups such as the disabled, the problems of the Third World, and the fearful potential of nuclear power. This overall crisis of conscience had a long-term effect on the design world. Although it appeared in a number of guises, from manifestoes to debates, social responsibility became an issue in all areas of design.

In graphic design it promoted an analytical approach to the communication of information, which gradually expanded by the late 1970s into the specialism of information design. The rapid development of new technology brought its own form of crisis and the 1970s shouldered the uneasy transfer from the hot metal tradition to computer typesetting, as well as the awkward phase when computer graphics and art could only be produced by, or with the aid of, a technician or scientist.

In spite of, or perhaps because of, the difficulties described Europe rose to an international lead in graphic design. Standardization and systemizing featured strongly in educational theory and professional practice, especially in Britain, Germany and Switzerland. European design groups such as Pentagram and Minale Tattersfield gained international reputations and design education also became a distinct European strength. Both spread European methods and ideas worldwide.

## Britain

Throughout the decade, Britain assumed a major role in European graphic design, advertising and design education (both at graduate and postgraduate level). The affluence of the 1960s was quickly replaced by a suffering British economy in the early 1970s. However, the cultural impetus of the 1960s was maintained and important advances occurred in both the educational and professional worlds.

Art education in Britain had been reorganized on a national level in the 1960s, and graphic design courses introduced in art colleges. (Prior to that, commercial art had existed in art schools but was taught within a heavy framework of arts and crafts.) After reorganization, art colleges produced the first generation of course-taught graphic designers who subsequently composed a solid profession in the 1970s. Art education was then taken over by a national degree validating body (the CNAA), which caused some art colleges to merge with polytechnics and absorb their academic structures. By the mid-1970s, graphic design had achieved both BA and MA degree status,

*British Airport Design, Minale Tattersfield, Britain, 1978.*

and was recognized as an academic study as well as a professional and technical training. An important advance, for graphic design is still pursued solely via technical training in many countries.

Academic foundations had also been laid in a number of other places. Michael Twyman had set up the Department of Typography and Graphic Communication in the University of Reading, which engaged in the teaching and research of all matters typographic. The Readability of Print Research Unit, based at the Royal College of Art and headed by Herbert Spencer, conducted research into the legibility of print and its publications (most notably the book *The Visible Word*) provided basic legibility guidelines for the new generation of art college graphic designers.

The existing seeds of academic research, the call for social responsibility in design, the information explosion and the arrival of new technology systems all contributed to the growth of information design as a specialism within graphic design. Information design concerned itself with the manner in which (often complex) information was presented to an intended audience, and through a research-and-analysis approach focused on issues such as the structuring of the information conveyed, the appropriateness of the communication medium, and the requirements or needs of the audience. In practice, information design brought new interest to the design of forms (such as tax forms), instructional information, teaching aids and other products of mass communication.

From a professional viewpoint the early 1970s saw the establishment of major design groups or partnerships formed by individuals who made it big in the 1950s and 1960s, and employing a workforce of the new art college graphic designers. This first generation of 'mega-groups' included the newly-formed Pentagram, Fitch and Co and Michael Peters and Partners, as well as existing groups such as Wolff Olins and Minale Tattersfield Partnership which had grown larger. The mood was go big, go international and even the older established groups followed: for example, Henrion Design Associates, still based largely around one personality, became HDA International in 1972.

Corporate design was in its most prolific phase in the 1970s. The concept of corporate identity was originally introduced to Britain in the 1950s by F. H. K. Henrion and Hans Schleger. It was mainly applied to the area of transport in the 1960s, closely followed by other public facilities (such as the Post Office) and reached its peak in the 1970s. Corporate identity programmes became the monopoly of the large design groups and, in rare cases, provided smaller or lesser known groups with instant exposure. Some of the better known examples are listed here (allowing for a bit of overflow on either side of the decade):

Blue Circle Cement (Henrion Design Associates)
Bovis Construction (Wolff Olins)

London Electricity Board (Henrion Design Associates)
British Petroleum (Crosby Fletcher Forbes)
British Airways (Negus & Negus)
C&A clothing stores (Henrion Design Associates)
WH Smith stationers (Guyatt Jenkins)
The Post Office (Banks and Miles)
British Airports Authority (Wolff Olins)
British Oxygen (BOC) (Wolff Olins)
Lucas Industries (Pentagram)
British Telecom (Banks and Miles)

*CAV and Girling packaging for Lucas Industries, Colin Forbes and Jean Robert, Pentagram, Britain.*

The graphic designers employed as the workforce for the design mega-groups gradually departed to form their own second generation mega-groups, such as Lloyd Northover, as well as smaller studios.

The 1970s proved to be an equally important decade for advertising in Britain. The London-based 'giants' of American advertising (such as J. Walter Thompson) now found tough competition from British ad agencies on the scene. At this time, British agencies produced bold, adventurous campaigns which demanded a new sophistication on the part of the reader-public. Conventions were challenged: in the late 1970s, the Clunk-Click seat belt campaign by Young & Rubicam brought sensationalism to public billboards. Cigarettes acquired a government warning on packs, were banned from television ads, and the advertising code of practice forbade the promotion and encouragement of cigarette smoking in print. Working within this constraint Collett, Dickenson Pearce broke ground with their advertising campaign for Benson and Hedges cigarettes – the launch of a subliminal approach which initially omitted brand names and later relied totally on association and mind play. Needless to say, other cigarette brands quickly followed suit but never quite matched the finesse of the original Benson and Hedges ads. However, this challenging new approach to communication in advertising also yielded high quality, artistic imagery, and British advertising was in a new class of its own.

The decade also unsettled a number of taboos (for example, the bra was first advertised on British TV in 1972) and saw the increase of advertising for public services and institutions. The advertising campaign for the Conservative Party in 1979 (Margaret Thatcher's election), with its image of the dole queue, made Saatchi & Saatchi a household name. Certain products, such as Guinness and Smirnoff Vodka, provided consistently entertaining campaigns.

Tremendous changes in technology in the 1970s caused a sort of identity crisis within the British graphic design profession, from which it has still not completely recovered. The transition period from hot metal to computer typesetting (generally termed 'phototypesetting') in the mid to late 1970s was not an easy one for Britain. The new systems of the late 1970s brought with them not only new specification rules (cap height versus body size) and terminology (leading = line feed) but also a totally new concept in typeface generation (digital systems), new typefaces adjusted specifically for computer generation, and last but not least, a whole new aesthetic. As if all that wasn't confusing enough, one company's system differed from another's, and all of the typesetting companies developed and changed their systems at a nightmarish pace.

Graphic designers just couldn't keep up. Four hot metal systems with one common form of specification had suddenly blossomed into double that number of computer systems (which would gradually grow to about forty), all with their own typeface drawings, specification, base unit, terminology and standard of quality. It was also common for one typeface to be known by different names under different systems. With Britain's classical typographic and print tradition, this was highly upsetting and many debates and conferences addressed themselves to the issue (and still do, by the way). For example, the Society of Typographic Designers debate at the Royal Society of Arts 1979, chaired by F. H. K. Henrion, centred on the motion 'This house believes that current photosetting techniques are undermining the basis of typographic design'. (The motion was defeated in the end, but not without a great deal of moaning.)

The popularization of personal home computers which weren't actually very easy to use (but once purchased, who had the nerve to admit it?), plus the introduction of public information systems such as Prestel, Oracle and Ceefax with their crude graphic imagery and lettering just about rounded off the new technology neurosis, graphically speaking. The neurosis pointed towards a new, freer generation of graphic designers – affectionately referred to as Letraset's Children by Henrion – who would be sadly devoid of certain well-loved traditions, such as the study of letterforms and calligraphy, the scholarly basis for choice of typefaces, the eye-to-hand craft of the ruling pen etc. But would it actually matter?

British graphic design also received an electric shock from another direction. The Punk movement of the late 1970s grew out of unemployment and youth unrest. Drugs and sex were its main props, and it was kept alive by pop groups such as the Sex Pistols. However, the pop groups were very much identified and promoted by a visual style, and the music industry yielded a new form of subversive graphics shown on record sleeves, pop concert posters and T-shirts. Fashion was also hit hard and the street-style generated by Punk (indeed, one of its most important facets) was captured in *i-D* magazine, (although launched in 1980) Terry Jones' *Not Another Punk Book*, and the music magazines. All acted as precursors to the 1980s magazines such as *i-D* and *The Face*, which contribute what little Britain has to offer to the avant-garde decade that follows.

# INTRODUCTION

The Readability of Print Research Unit was set up at the Royal College of Art in 1966 to investigate problems of legibility in information publishing. An initial grant from the International Publishing Corporation resulted in the publication of what is now a standard work on legibility, Herbert Spencer's *The Visible Word*.

In the early 1970s the Office for Scientific and Technical Information provided funding for a series of studies on the ways in which the legibility of printed text and numerals is affected by poor quality reproduction. This was followed by work for the British Library Research and Development Department (formerly OSTI) on the design of typewritten and typeset catalogues and bibliographies. Subsequent grants enabled this work to be extended to deal with catalogues on microfiche and on Prestel. This increasing concern with other media in addition to print led to the Unit's name being changed to 'Graphic Information Research Unit' in 1978. Meanwhile there were also studies of signing and guiding in libraries and museums, culminating in the publication of a design manual for librarians in 1981.

A study on the legibility of Prestel displays, carried out for The Post Office (now British Telecom) in 1978, highlighted the many problems resulting from the increasing need to transfer information freely from one medium to another. These problems are more pressing now than ever before, but the Research Unit ceased to function in 1981 through lack of funding.

Municipal and regional pride in Germany at this time created vast opportunities for the design of civic identities, such as the Berlin identity by Anton Stankowski. A new corporate programme was introduced by Deutsche Post (German Post Office) in 1977. Curiously enough, DB or Deutsche Bundesbahn (German Federal Railways) has still not updated its graphic identity from the 1950s, apparently waiting for a new overall European standard to appear

The 1970s also found Germany as one of the world leaders in the production of typesetting equipment, through companies such as Berthold and Stempel. Leading German type designers of the time included Günter Lange, Design Director of Berthold and designer of many typefaces for Berthold; Erik Spiekerman, then living in Britain but also producing typefaces for Berthold and representative of the new younger generation dedicated to photosetting and oblivious to the decline of hot metal; and Hermann Zapf, responsible over the years for such typeface classics as Aldus, Palatino, Melior, Optima, Zapf Book, Zapf International and Zapf Chancery – all licensed internationally.

## The Netherlands

The graphic design community of The Netherlands was growing from strength to strength during this period, and younger groups began to provide healthy competition for the well established Total Design in Amsterdam. In 1967 an industrial design studio in the Hague took on the name of Tel Design Associates and acquired a Graphic Design Department founded by Gert Dumbar. Dumbar was responsible for the department's first large and complex commission, the corporate identity for Nederlandse Spoorwegen (Dutch Railways), involving a complete house style, railway-guides, timetables, pictogrammes, signage plans on railway stations, logotype, colour system and railway station interiors. The scheme was widely acclaimed for its clear, rational handling of information and vibrant use of colour – and the bright yellow carriages are still the most exciting feature of the national railway system today. (Incidentally, the annual pocket timetable book from this scheme is one of the best-selling books in The Netherlands.) Largely due to the Dutch Railways identity, The Netherlands gained world attention in the 1970s as the source of new developments in graphic design.

In 1977, Gert Dumbar parted from Tel and established his own Studio Dumbar in the Hague, which then collaborated with Total Design on the complete housestyle for ptt (The Dutch Post Office). Innovation became the hallmark of Studio Dumbar, and their work was characterized by an element of surprise in the form of humour, emotion, or the fantastic – whether applied to theatre posters or signage in hospital corridors. Their popularity and position are magnified in the 1980s as The Netherlands becomes a hotbed for the avant-garde.

## Germany

Graphic design in Germany during the 1970s was largely devoted to corporate identity and systematization. Otl Aicher was the undisputed master of corporate programmes and a central figure in German post-war graphic design. One of the founder members of the Hochschule für Gestaltung Ulm and its Director in the early 1960s, Aicher achieved worldwide recognition for his pictogrammes and corporate identity for the Munich Olympic Games in 1972. (In America he has been called the Father of Geometric Man!) His corporate schemes included Braun, Lufthansa, Westdeutsche Landesbank, Blohm & Voss, Erco, an information system for Frankfurt airport, and others. At the end of the decade Aicher applied his well-known, clean geometric style to a corporate design for the German town of Isny, producing a series of geometric images of extra-ordinary warmth and beauty. (Thereby disproving the popular theory that Hard-edge = Boring.)

Rolf Müller, who studied at Ulm and worked with Aicher on the Munich Olympiad project, set up his own commercially successful studio in Munich and has also made extensive use of modular design, grids, and a clean geometric style. His projects include the Leverkusen town identity programme, and exhibitions and corporate work for the municipality of Bonn and the University of Regensberg.

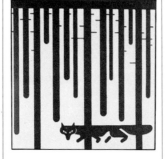

*Pictograms for the town of Isny,*
*'Otl Aicher, W.Germany, c.1979.*

## Switzerland

The Swiss Design Movement, with its formalized methods and principles, was now well established throughout the world. Mainstream graphic design in Switzerland was still under the heavy influence of leading figures of the 1960s. Josef Müller-Brockmann, for example, was responsible for the corporate identity scheme of the SBB (Swiss Federal Railways) in the late 1970s.

However, interesting off-shoots were also apparent in the 1970s. The work of the small design team Odermatt & Tissi (a man and a woman) was based in the 1960s Swiss hard-edge style, but incorporated a more lively and colourful approach. While at the Kunstgewerbeschule Basle an instructor named Wolfgang Weingart was leading a rather wild departure from the recognizable Swiss ethic. Weingart's highly experimental approach was basically a typographic exploration based on joining two contrasting worlds: objectivity (Swiss hard-edge, programming, grids) versus subjectivity (passion, emotion, irreverence). With a constant intake of American students to the Basle school, Weingart taught his innovative approach to the next generation of American designers (including April Greiman, who joins him as one of the leading avant garde personalities of the 1980s).

## The United States

The Swiss Design Movement had made a tremendous impact on USA graphic design in the late 1960s and early 1970s. But the 1970s progressed to show a variety of styles and influences at work across the country, including American folk art, Art Nouveau/psychedelic pastiche, 1950s commercial art, Swiss hard-edge and, later in the decade, Swiss hard-edge gone haywire (New Wave) practised mainly on the West Coast.

An essential name to the 1970s was the International Typeface Corporation, or ITC. In 1970 ITC was established in New York as a licensing house for typefaces, with the aim of providing new typefaces for the new technology (i.e. phototypesetting manufacturers). In order to popularize ITC typefaces among designers, a style catalogue cum magazine was distributed worldwide named *U & lc* (Upper and Lowercase) with Herb Lubalin as Editorial Design Director. Lubalin's love of decorative lettering and illustrative style was reflected in *U & lc*, and the extensive variety of new and often decorative typefaces offered by ITC produced an initial jolt to European designers used to Germanic severity. But acceptance came gradually with time and *U & lc*, with its technological articles and updates, certainly did its best to help smooth the pathway to computer typesetting around the world.

Another important name to the decade was Massimo Vignelli. He co-founded Unimark International Corporation for Design and Marketing (1965) and in 1966 designed a sign system for the New York Subway. He then established Vignelli Associates in 1971 (with his architect wife Lella) and subsequent projects included the redesign of the New York City Subway map (1972) and the graphics system for the Washington Metro (1976).

The unpopular Vietnam War dragged on into the 1970s and the stream of protest posters continued, including the classic 'Q. And babies? A. And babies.'. On the bright side – Buckminster Fuller, with his concept of Spaceship Earth, and Victor Papanek, author of 'Design for the Real World', brought ecology and Third World problems to the attention of design students all over America. With a little help from the world oil crisis concern for the environment gradually spread to the international design community.

1

Batchelors
SOUP MIXES
THICK ONION
MAKES 1 GALLON

6

JOHN WEST dressed crab
'MIDDLE CUT' BRAND  43g net 1½ oz
PRODUCT OF SCOTLAND

3

JOHN WEST Skippers
'MIDDLE CUT' BRAND  Smoked brisling in tomato sauce
TRY SKIPPER HORS D'OEUVRE SEE BACK FOR RECIPE
PRODUCT OF NORWAY

4

Knorr Florida Spring Vegetable Soup
3p OFF YOUR NEXT PURCHASE (see over)
Swiss Recipe

Batchelors Cup-a-Soup
Onion & Beef Soup
INSTANT just add boiling water
4 single serving sachets

7

Lyons Maid
Lemon Sorbet
a tangy, refreshing water ice
CONTENTS: 4·3 fl. oz. (122 c.c.) Lyons Maid Limited Glacier House Hammersmith Grove London W6 0NG

2

McVitie's
A McVITIE-CADBURY PRODUCT
Mini Pies
Two Apple & Blackcurrant

5

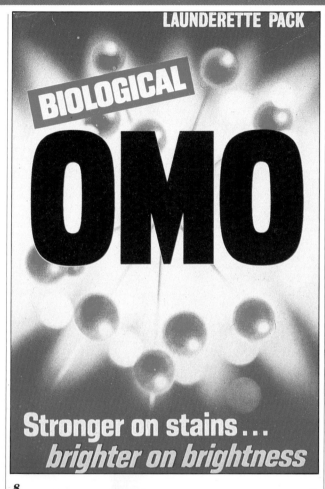

**LAUNDERETTE PACK**

**BIOLOGICAL OMO**

**Stronger on stains...**
*brighter on brightness*

8

*Mild und leicht mit feinen Brasiltabaken*

HANDELSGOLD

**BRASIL-ZIGARILLOS NR. 154**

Der Bundesgesundheitsminister:
**Rauchen gefährdet
Ihre Gesundheit**

9

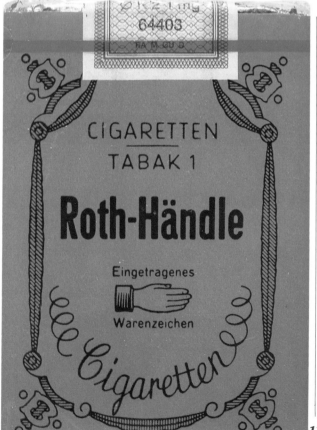

10

CIGARETTEN
TABAK 1

**Roth-Händle**

Eingetragenes

Warenzeichen

*Cigaretten*

11

**1** *Batchelors soup mixes packaging, Britain, 1975.*
**2** *Lyons Maid sorbet packaging, Britain, 1971.* **3** *John West tinned fish packaging, Britain, 1975.* **4** *John West tinned fish packaging, Britain, 1975.*
**5** *McVitie's pie packaging, Britain, 1975.* **6** *Knorr soup packaging, Britain, 1973.*
**7** *Batchelors soup packaging, Britain, 1975.* **8** *Omo soap powder packaging, Britain, 1970s.* **9** *Biba packaging, Pentagram, Britain, 1970s.*
**10** *Handelsgold cigarette packaging, Brazil/Germany, 1970s.* **11** *Roth-Händle cigarette packaging, Germany, 1970s.*

# ADVERTISEMENTS

## 29th Oct. 1991

Just a small reminder that, according to statistics, anyone buying a new Volvo today will probably have to replace it on the above date.

**VOLVO**

Source: A recent Swedish Government survey showed that the average life Volvo is still around sixteen years later.

**1**

## At around 90°F, workers evaporate.

65°F. He's okay.　72°F. He's feeling warm.　78°F. He's hot and bothered.

80°F. He can't concentrate.　85°F. He's fading fast.　90°F. He's disappeared.

**People work better in Colt conditions.**

**2**

Is this the only difference between the American and British businessmen?

**4**

## What makes a cigarette so enjoyable?

**Hydrogen Cyanide.**

**Ammonia.**

**Carbon Monoxide.**

**Nicotine.**

**Butane.**

**Tar.**

**Phenol.**

**5**

---

**1** Volvo newspaper advertisement, art director Phil Mason, Britain, 1976. **2** Colt International newspaper advertisement, art director John Wood, Britain, 1976. **3** Parker Pen advertisement, art director Neil Godfrey, Britain, 1976. **4** Colt International newspaper advertisement, art director Philip Gough, Britain, 1971. **5** Health Education Council newspaper advertisement, art director John Hegarty, Britain, 1971. **6** Volkswagen newspaper advertisement, art director Brian Byfield, Britain, 1971.

---

## How Parker conquered the little things that made you hate the fountain pen.

We have always regretted the decline of the fountain pen.

The little perisher.

Not, as you may smilingly suppose, because our fortunes declined with it.

Parker pens have always sold well.

But because, for us, the fountain pen symbolises an unhurried, civilised way of life.

Ball-pens are fine for scribbling notes and jotting down figures.

But somehow it still seems more polite to write a personal letter with a fountain pen, and to write a poem with anything else would surely be sacrilegious.

Unfortunately, it takes us such a long time to build each Parker pen that very few can afford one.

To this day most people don't know the joy of owning a pen that doesn't blot, scratch, dry-up or leak.

A pen that glides over the page leaving shining, wet words behind it. Such a pen, in fact, as our latest, the Parker Cirrus finished in rolled gold.

At £18 you'll be glad to hear that it suffers from none of the faults that still haunt other fountain pens.

Its ink sac won't perish because we now make it of plastic, not rubber.

Nor will it puncture for we have protected it with an inner barrel of stainless steel and dispensed with those filling levers, buttons and plungers which can do such injury to it.

(Moreover, you can replace the ink-sac with a cartridge of Quink whenever you want to simply by un-screwing it.)

The clip of the Cirrus is of rolled gold on phosphor bronze. It shouldn't snap or lose tension.

The loser.

We can also promise that you'll never get a pocketful of ink or a blotted copy book. Because below the nib we've designed a finned ink collector which controls the flow of ink whatever the conditions.

The permanent 'understain'.

Even when the heat of your hand or the increased pressure of flying at high altitudes causes the air in the pen to expand, the rush of ink won't get further than the collector.

But of course it is scratchy nibs on which owners of fountain pens traditionally vent their wrath.

We build our nibs from sheets of pure 14 carat gold which we cut, press and persuade into a shape that perfectly conveys the ink to the tip.

Believe it or not, this operation consists of fifteen separate stages, many of which are by hand, and scrutinised under microscopes.

The tip of the nib must be stronger than gold, of course, and the alloy we use, Plathenium, is actually four times harder than steel and ten times smoother.

There are eight styles and if you find you're unhappy with the one you choose, we'll change it for another grade within a month of purchase.

You'll notice that we have left the looks of the new Cirrus to last. But we have in fact spent a great deal of time and reflection on how to make it look and feel right in your hand.

Scratching a living.

Whether you think any other pen looks better, however, is a question of taste.

But we can assure you that no other pen writes better.

**PARKER**

THE PARKER CIRRUS COSTS £18 THERE IS ALSO A MATCHING CIRRUS BALL PEN AND PROPELLING PENCIL IN EACH RECOMMENDED RETAIL PRICES INCLUDING VAT.

**3**

Why don't they ever sit on Volkswagens?

**6**

### "A new Eurodollar idea? At a time like this?"

As luck would have it, we seem to have launched our floating rate Eurobond at a most depressing time.

Which in many ways is just the exactly the right time to launch an idea like this.

If it takes off now, while the market's down in the dumps, imagine how it'll go when the market's back to its old self again.

A ray of hope was how the Times described the idea (On the day that the Eurobond market slid to a record low).

And as fixed rate issues were being postponed right, left and centre, our first floating rate issue was over-subscribed by nearly $100m.

A fair measure of its appeal.

Not that we invented it purely and simply with a falling market in mind.

Months ago at our merchant bank subsidiary (Bankers Trust International) we weighed up all the shortcomings of the fixed rate bond. And decided there was nothing wrong that a little ingenuity couldn't put right.

In a moment of inspiration, we hit on the floating rate note. Which is adjusted every six months in line with London interbank interest rates.

At the best of times, it makes the Eurobond a more attractive all-round proposition.

At worst, the flexible coupon means

there'll still be buyers for the bonds.

It's an idea that's typical of the way we think and work.

If there's a better way to do something we try to be among the first to find it. Whether it's in merchant banking or commercial banking.

Talk to Dmitri de Gunzburg or David Date at Bankers Trust International (Tel 01-588-7131) Or to Ken Prescot here at Bankers Trust (Tel 01-248-3251)

At a time like this, a few new ideas may be just what the doctor ordered.

Bankers Trust. ▲

**7**

### What you'd need to read every day if you didn't read Newsweek once a week.

If you can't afford to rely on the news reported from one country's point of view, read Newsweek once a week.

**Newsweek**
THE INTERNATIONAL NEWSMAGAZINE
*History in the making.*

**8**

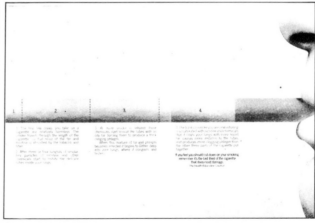

**9**

**7** *Bankers Trust Company newspaper advertisement, art director Martyn Walsh, Britain, 1971.*

**8** *Newsweek International magazine advertisement, art director John Hegarty, 1976.*
**9** *Health Education Council*

*newspaper advertisement, art director John Hegarty, Britain, 1971.*

# POSTERS

1

2

1 Architectural exhibition poster, Stedelijk Museum, Wim Crouwel, Holland, 1975.

2 'Perfidia', Gert Dumbar, Holland, c.1971. 3 Bally shoes poster, Barnard Villemot,

3

4

British Painting '74 Hayward Gallery
Arts Council of Great Britain 26 September to 17 November 1974
Monday to Friday 10 to 8/Saturdays 10 to 6/Sundays 12 to 6
Admission 30p/Children, students and pensioners 15p
10p all day Monday and between 6 to 8 Tuesdays to Fridays

5

France, 1970s. **4** Bally shoes poster, Bernard Villemot, France, 1970. **5** 'British Painting 74', Arts Council exhibition poster, Alan Fletcher for Pentagram, Britain, 1974.

**6** Henry Moore poster, Henryk Tomaszewski, Poland, 1962. **7** 'Avec L'Enfant', Roman Cieslewicz, France, 1978.

6

AVEC L'ENFANT

LE COMITE        MONTREUILLOIS        DE L'ANNEE        DE L'ENFANT

7 | 153

# MAGAZINES AND JOURNALS

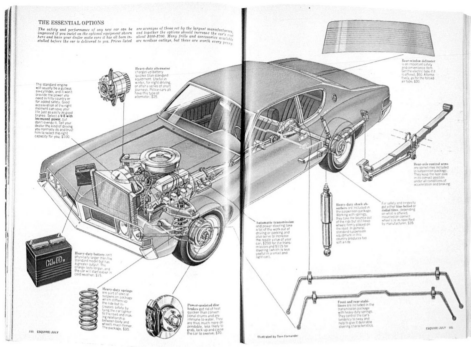

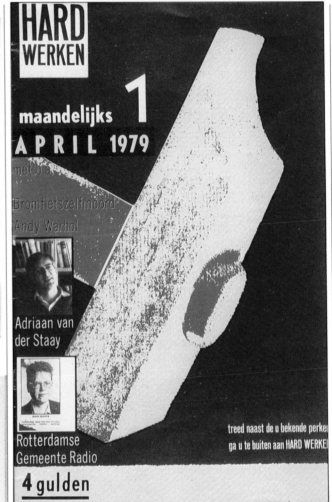

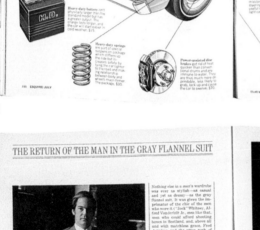

*1 & 2 Spread from Esquire, art director Jean-Paul Goude, US, July 1972. 3 Hard Werken no.* 1, Hard Werken design group, Holland, 1979. *4 Esquire cover, art director Jean-Paul* Goude, US, July 1972. *5 Hard Werken no. 3, Hard Werken design group, Holland, 1979.*

i-D

PRINTED BY AND AVAILABLE FROM BETTER BADGES
286 PORTOBELLA R'D, LONDON W10. 60p+25p P+P
ALSO FROM I.D.-71 SHERRIFF R'D LONDON NW6.

Nº 2

I.D. Is a Fashion/Style Magazine.Style isn't what but how you wear clothes.Fashion is the way you walk,talk,dance and prance.Through I.D. ideas travel fast and free of the mainstream - so join us on the run.

WHATS IN

STRAIGHT UP:Every issue includes a report,from your open-air catwalk the street.We snap and chat to you,the Model.This issue visits:Kensington M'kt,The Kings R'd,Blackbull R'd,Euston R'd and Camden Lock M'kt. CON-FIDE:What happened? S.J. was sewing on buttons at the age of three. She became a Bodysnatcher-now th band has split and she admits "I'm just a hippy at heart".
MEANWHILE ON THE OTHER SIDE OF TOWN:Spandau Ballet,the facts behind the how to make it big story.the right time for Reformation.

RENT A DRESS:Girl for all reasons,lovely Jayne Chilcs explores the unknown and discovers Theatrical Costume Hire Agencies have bottomless trunks.
LONDON LOOKS:A foreign 'body'shops around for a second skin that says it all-attracting other bodies whilst fooling the antibodies.Circulate,survive. HAT CHECK:Steve 'Mad Hatter' Jones,presents crowns he designs for the Kings and Queens of Londons nightworld.Never failing to cap them all. DO-WHAT:Reports from the stage on which you perform-where to go,what to do.In this issue:Gaz's Rockin Blues-Reggae n' Roll,A Rock n' Roll cafe "Down the Holloway R'd".Hell today gone tomorrow.An Ark Ent Event at the venue and Fr-I.D-ays thats I.D. nite when you can meet mag and pose,perform and dance for the camera.
BRIGHT SPARKS:Ideas and information-Willy Brown a Modern Classic in profile,M's Official Secret,Acme Acting-"Doorbell rings,performance beg-ins,Karate classes-Mugger mashing exercises etc etc............ OUT OF ORDER:Wake up Albion-Hideous visions of Eurostyle penetrate our shops"a point of view.Plus Readers Writes-A letters page............

6

7

**6** *i-D magazine, (back cover of issue no. 2), art editor Terry Jones, Britain, 1980.* **7** *Spread from Nova, art director David Hillman, Britain, 1973.*
**8** *HBG magazine, house magazine for insurance company, Tel Design, Holland, 1971.*

HOME IS WHERE THE HEAT IS

hbg magazine 2

8

# MAGAZINES AND JOURNALS

1

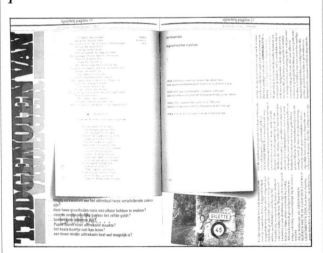

4

5

## Ist diese Typografie noch zu retten?

**Oder leben wir auf dem Mond? Is This Typography Worth Supporting, Or Do We Live On The Moon?** A special selection from the works of Weingart from 1969–1976. Thoughts and observations of a friend. And personal comments from the author.

2

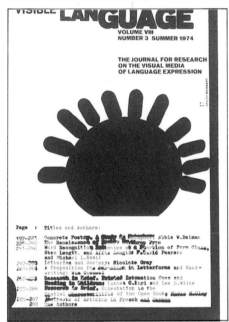

3

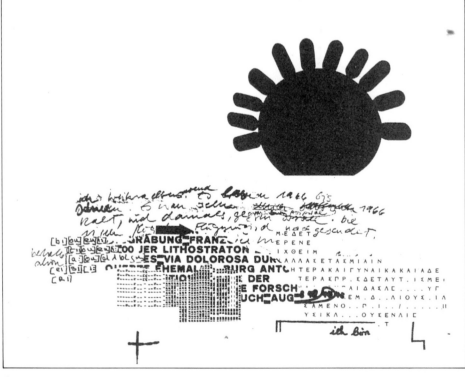

6

7

8

9

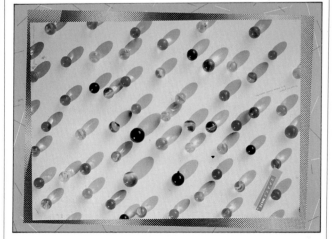

10

*1 Spread from i-D magazine, Terry Jones, Britain, 1970.*
*2 Special edition of Typografische Monatsblätter magazine, Wolfgang Weingart, Switzerland, 1976. 3 Visible Language journal, cover by Wolfgang Weingart, US, 1974.*
*4 & 5 Spreads from Lijsterbrij magazine, Holland, 1972-73.*
*6 Collage detail from special edition of Typografische Monatsblätter, Wolfgang Weingart, Switzerland,*

*December 1976. 7 Cal Arts (California Institute of the Arts) folder-poster, April Greiman and Jayme Odgers, US, 1978.*
*8 & 9 'Spacemats', April Greiman and Jayme Odgers, US, 1978. 10 'Spacemats', April Greiman and Jayme Odgers, US, 1978.*

**Amsterdam tourist and shopping information**

SKILFUL CYCLING

OSLO *Norway*

**1** *Habitat by Post catalogue, Britain, early 1970s.*
**2** *Amsterdam tourist and shopping information leaflet, WV-Amsterdam Tourist Association, Holland, early 1970s.* **3** *Skilful cycling manual, Royal Society for the Prevention of Accidents, Britain, 1970.* **4** *Norwegian tourist information brochure, Oslo Travel Association, Norway, 1974.*

2

3

4

# BOOKS

**STEVENSON TREASURE ISLAND**

CONTENTS: HISTORY OF TREASURE ISLAND. MAP OF SAME SHOWING WHERE THE TREASURE WAS BURIED. THE CREW REGISTER. AND PLAN OF THE HISPANIOLA. MOST COMMON SEAFARING VESSELS OF THE 18TH CENTURY. FIREARMS AND SHIPS TACKLE. THE SECRET STATUTES OF THE BUCCANEERS AND A GREAT DEAL MORE. TOGETHER WITH A CHART MARKING THE POSITION OF SEVERAL WRECKS WHOSE PRICELESS TREASURES STILL AWAIT DISCOVERY BY MEN OF GREAT DARING AND ADVENTURE

1

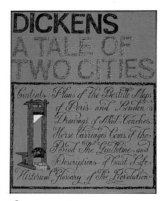

**FENIMORE COOPER THE LAST OF THE MOHICANS**

Contents. Plans of Forts. English and French weapons. Uniforms. Canoes. Indian foods. Animals & birds. Map of Tribal Reservations & a Glossary of American Indian life

2

**DICKENS A TALE OF TWO CITIES**

Contents: Plans of the Bastille Maps of Paris and London. Drawings of Mail Coaches. Horse Carriages. Coins of the Period. The Guillotine. and Descriptions of Court Life. Historical Glossary of The Revolution

3

**1** 'Treasure Island' by Robert Louis Stevenson, Studio Vista Books, Britain, 1973. **2** 'The Last of the Mohicans' by Fenimore Cooper, cover by Christopher Bradbury, Studio Vista Books, Britain, 1973. **3** 'A Tale of Two Cities' by Charles Dickens, Studio Vista Books, Britain, 1973.

**4** Spread from 'Treasure Island', Studio Vista Books, Britain, 1973. **5** Spread from 'The Last of the Mohicans', Christopher Bradbury, Studio Vista Books, Britain, 1973. **6** Front cover of 'The Last Whole Earth Catalog', US, 1970s.

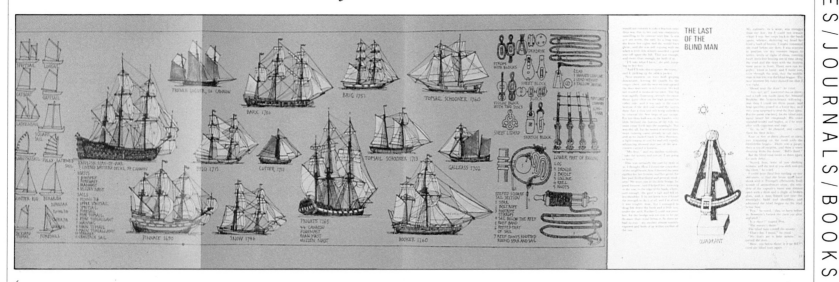

4

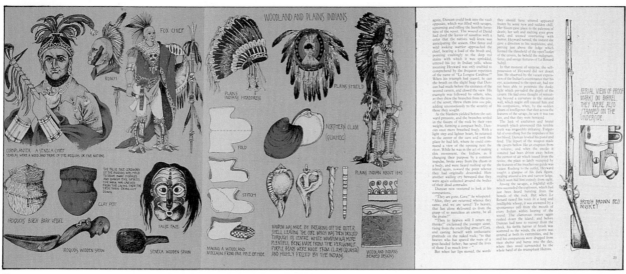

5

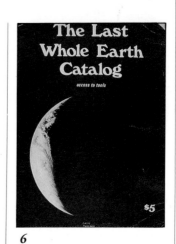

6

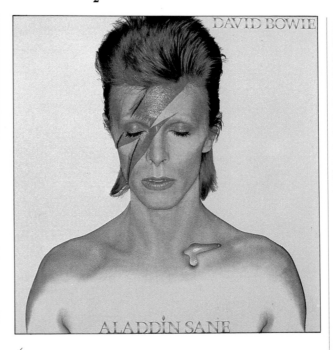

1 'Never Mind the Bollocks, here's the Sex Pistols', Virgin Records, Britain, 1977.
2 'Yesterday's', Atlantic Records, Britain, early 1970s.
3 'Soul Power', ABC Records, Germany. 4 'Aladdin Sane', David Bowie, cover by Duffy and Delia Philo, RCA Records, Britain, 1973. 5 'Into the Purple Valley', Ry Cooder, Reprise Records, US, 1970s.

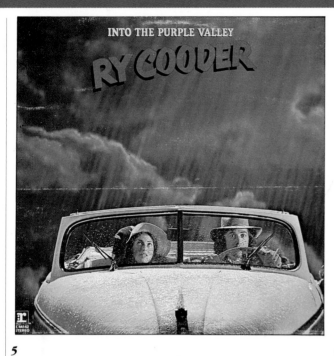

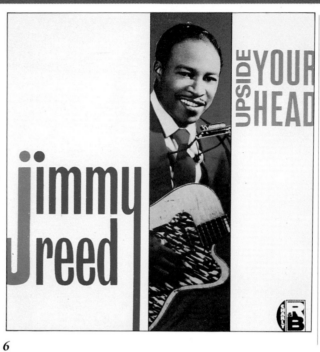

5

6

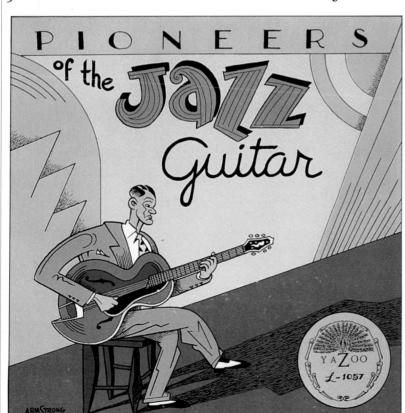

7

8

# SYMBOLS AND TRADEMARKS

 1

 5

 9

 1

 2

 6

 10

 1

 3

 7

 11

 15

 4

 8

 12

 1

**17**

**21**

**26**

**28**

**18**

**TONIO'S**

**22**

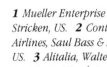

**27**

**23**

**19**

**24**

**20**

**25**

**1** Mueller Enterprise Inc, Jack Stricken, US. **2** Continental Airlines, Saul Bass & Associates, US. **3** Alitalia, Walter Landor Associates, US. **4** Royal Bank of Scotland, Mark Woodham, for Allied International Designers Ltd, Britain. **5** American Telephone and Telegraph, Saul Bass & Associates, US, 1971. **6** International Wool Secretariat, Francesco Saroglia, Italy. **7** ELAL Israel Airlines, Otto Treumann, US. **8** Expo 70, Takeshi Otaka, Japan. **9** Robert Leicht Brewery, Nelly Rudin, Switzerland. **10** Barkon Petroleum Inc, Primo Angeli, US. **11** Oklahoma City's Liberty National bank & Trust Company, Walter Landor Associates, US, 1971. **12** Cotton Inc, Walter Landor Associates, US, 1973. **13** Pan Am, Joseph Montgomery, US. **14** Parker Adult Games, Arnold Arnold, US, 1972. **15** Quaker Oats Company, Saul Bass & Associates, US, 1971. **16** AMF, Anspach, Grossman, Portugal Inc, US. **17** KLM Airlines, Holland, F.H.K.Henrion, Britain. **18** National Hockey League Players Association, Lee Payne, US, 1972. **19** 'Goat's Head Soup' record logo for Rolling Stones, US. **20** Exxon, Raymond Loewy/William Snaith Inc, US, 1973. **21** Pepsi-Cola Company, Gould & Co. Inc, US, 1969. **22** Tonio's Restaurant, Saul Bass & Associates, US. **23** Levi Strauss Company, Walter Landor Associates, US, 1969. **24** General Telephone & Electronics, Arnold Copeland, US, 1971. **25** 'I Love New York' badge, Milton Glaser, US. **26** Jai-Alai pelota court, Bud Jarrin for Milton Roth, US. **27** L'eggs, Hanes Corporation, US, 1969. **28** Green Giant Company, Lippincott & Margulies, US, 1970.

# INFORMATION DESIGN

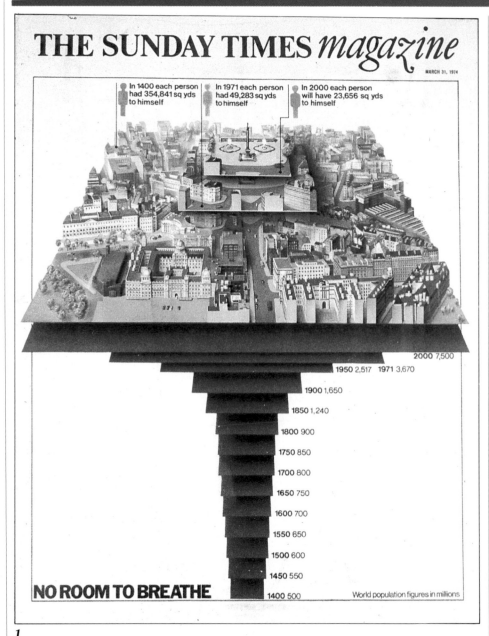

**THE SUNDAY TIMES** *magazine*

MARCH 31, 1974

In 1400 each person had 354,841 sq yds to himself

In 1971 each person had 49,283 sq yds to himself

In 2000 each person will have 23,656 sq yds to himself

2000 7,500
1950 2,517  1971 3,670
1900 1,650
1850 1,240
1800 900
1750 850
1700 800
1650 750
1600 700
1550 650
1500 600
1450 550
1400 500

**NO ROOM TO BREATHE**

World population figures in millions

*1*

*1 Variation of a bar chart by QED, Sunday Times magazine, Britain, 1974. 2 Flow diagram by QED showing beer making process, Macdonald guideline series, Britain, 1970s. 3 Olympic Pictogrammes, Otl Aicher, Germany, 1972. 4 Pages from 'The Yearbook', Japan, 1974.*

*5 Dinosaurs and Prehistoric Life leaflet, The Diagram Group, Britain.*

164

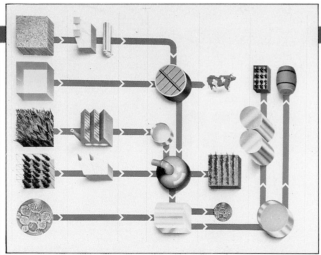

*2*

*3*

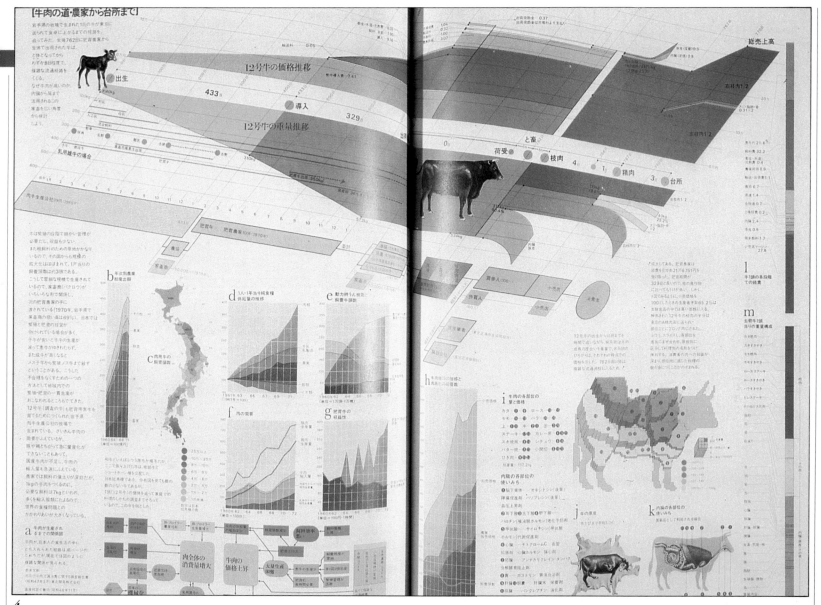

**4**

**5**

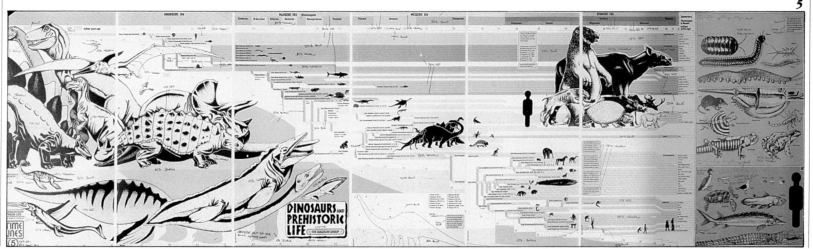

# INFORMATION DESIGN

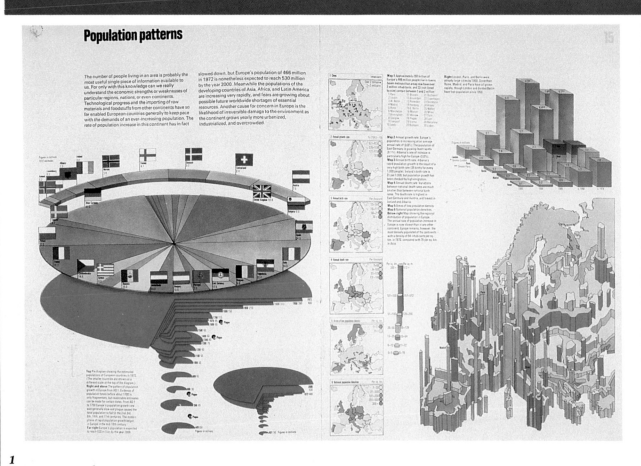

**1** Spread from Europe, Caxton Publishing Company, Coventure Ltd, Britain, 1973.
**2** Diagram from Eisenbahnen Atlas, O.S.Nock, Delphin Verlag/ Rand McNally Company, 1978. **3** Spread from Longman Atlas of Modern British History, Campbell/ Kinsey Group, Britain, 1978.

**1**

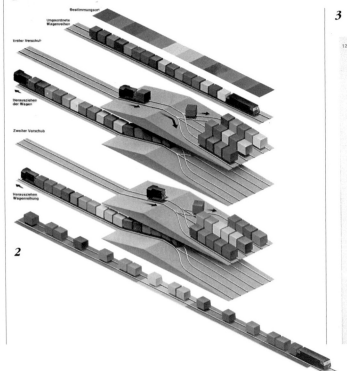

**2**

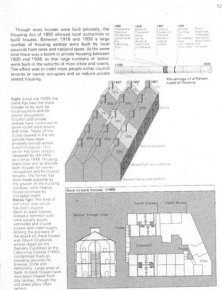

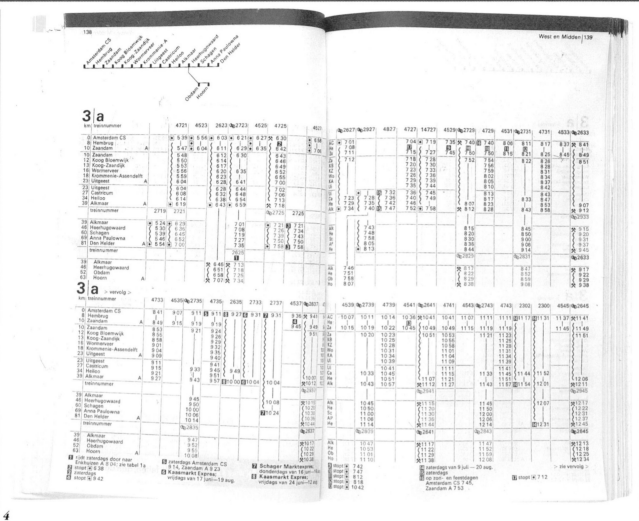

**4** Spread from pocket book of Netherlands Railway timetables, Studio Dumbar, Holland, 1977-78. **5** Moving Card, Studio Dumbar. **6** Pocket book of Netherlands Railway timetables, Studio Dumbar, Holland, 1974-75. **7** Pocket book of Netherlands Railway timetables, Studio Dumbar, Holland, 1977-78.
**8** Information design journal.

# INFORMATION DESIGN

**1**

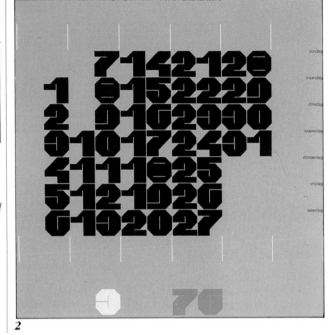

**2**

**3**

**1 & 3** *Mart Spruijt (printers)
calendar, Jan van Toorn,
Holland, 1971-72.* **2** *Grey and
Black calendar, Holland,
1976.* **4** *Detail from
'Gobbledegook', showing
redesign of DHSS form.*
**5** *'Gobbledegook', a critical
review of official forms and
leaflets, National Consumer
Council, 1980.*

---

### Form 4

DEPARTMENT OF HEALTH AND SOCIAL SECURITY

(DHSS)

(LO address) ┌ Davenport House, Hulme Place,
The Crescent,
Salford. M5 4PA ┐

Tel 061-736 5888 Ext 204

Ref No

5810/                                        19

Mr /Mrs /Miss ............................

...................................................

...................................................

...................................................

Your appointment is

on ........................(Date) at ................(Time)

PLEASE ARRIVE AT THE OFFICE PROMPTLY AS IT MAY
BE DIFFICULT TO FIT IN ANOTHER APPOINTMENT THE
SAME DAY IF YOU ARRIVE LATE. Do not wait to see the
receptionist but go straight to the waiting room until you are
called for interview at Booth number..................

#### What you need to bring with you

SO THAT YOUR PROPER ENTITLEMENT TO SUPPLE-
MENTARY BENEFIT CAN BE DECIDED YOU MUST
PROVIDE EVIDENCE ABOUT YOUR CIRCUMSTANCES.
YOU SHOULD THEREFORE BRING ANY OF THE
FOLLOWING ITEMS YOU HAVE FOR YOURSELF, YOUR
WIFE, OR ANY DEPENDANTS:-

Form B1 or B1C from the Unemployment Benefit Office if
unemployed (unless already submitted).

Last two wage slips.

Letter from employer if holding a week's wages in hand.

Form A 165
(Env EW 58F)                            Please turn over

### Supplementary benefit

**Please come in and see us about
supplementary benefit on**

_____

at _____

Please come in on time. If you are late, we
may not be able to give you a new time on
the same day.

When you come in, please go to the waiting
room. Wait till your name is called out.

**If you cannot come in at the right
time,** ring up and tell us. The number is at
the bottom of this letter.

Please read the list on the back of this letter.
We need to see the things on it to work
out your benefit. If you forget to bring
them, it could hold up your benefit.

Please turn over →

Social Security Office
Davenport House
Hulme Place
The Crescent
Salford M5 4PA.
Phone 736 5888 line

A165 in E/SFU                        Date

**4**

---

### GOBBLEDEGOOK

By Tom Vernon for the National Consumer Council. A critical review of official forms and leaflets—and how to improve them

With reference to your claim for a
supplementary allowance, the Sup-
lementary Benefits Commission
hereby notify you that provided your
circumstances remain unchanged
(see paragraphs 2 and 3 overleaf)
and you remain registered for work
at an Employment Office you are
entitled to a supplementary allowance
of an amount which, when added to
any unemployment benefit (including
any earnings related supplement) to
which you may be entitled, will equal
the amount shown for the first of the
benefit pay weeks stated opposite.

Weekly payments will continue at the
rate(s) shown unless before any such
payment is made there has been a
relevant change in your circumstances
or you have failed to claim benefit for
a full benefit pay week.

**5**

# TYPOGRAPHY

**1**

**2**

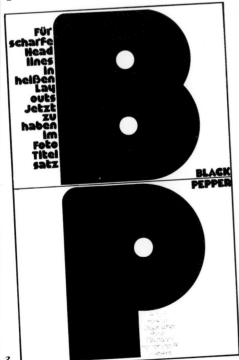

**3**

**4**

**5**

*1 & 2* Hollenstein Phototype,
Hans-Rudolf Lutz, France,
c.1973. *3 & 4* Alphabet for
film setting of titles, Peter
Steiner, Germany, c.1973.
*5* Technical review for Alfieri &
Lacroix, Franco Grignani for
Studio Grignani, Italy, c.1973.

# TYPOGRAPHY

ABCDEFGHIJKLMNOPQRSTUVWXYZ

1234567890 &?!£$(.,;:)

ABCDEFGHIJKLMNOPQRSTUVWXYZ
abcdefghijklmnopqrstuvwxyz    1234567890

ABCDEFGHIJKLMNOPQRSTUVWXYZ
KLMNOPQRSTUVWXYZ

abcdefghijklmnopqrstuvwxyz    $1234567890

ABCDEFGHIJKLMNOPQRSTUVWXYZ

abcdefghijklmnopqrstuvwxyz

1234567890

ABCDEFGHIJKLMNOPQRSTUVWXYZÆŒ
abcdefghijklmnopqrstuvwxyz

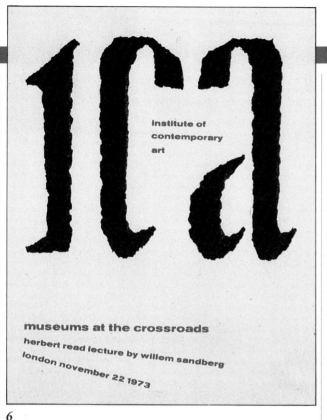

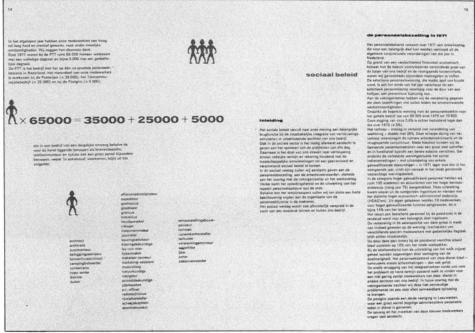

**6** *Poster for lecture, Institute of Contemporary Arts, London, Sandberg, 1973.* **7** *'Wilhelm Wagenfeld', Kunstgewerbtmuseum, Cologne, Sandberg, 1973.* **8** *Cobra & Contrasts, Detroit Institute of Arts, Sandberg, 1974.* **9** *Pages from ptt report, Sandberg, 1974.*

1

2

4

3

5

**1, 2 & 3** *British Commonwealth Games stamps, 1/9, 1/6 and 5d, 1970.* **4, 5, 6 & 7** *Dutch stamps, Jan van Toorn, Holland, 1979.*

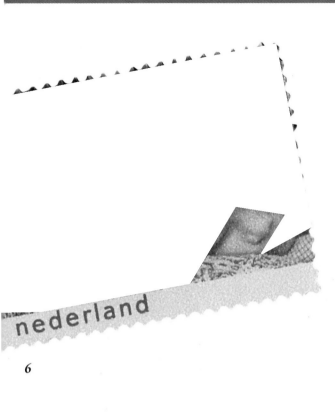

nederland

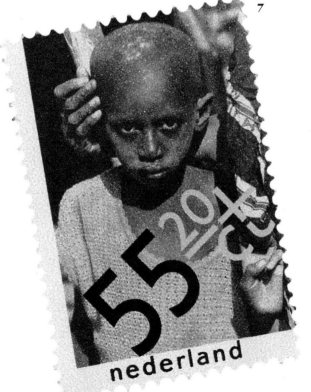

nederland

8 *Tutankhamun discovery 1922, 3d stamp, Britain, 1972.* 9 *Australian Natives Association, Richard Beck, 6c stamp, Australia, 1971.* 10 *Postcode stamps, Rene van Raalte and Gert Dumbar, Holland, 1978.* **11 & 12** *Banknote, Sri Lanka, 1970s.*

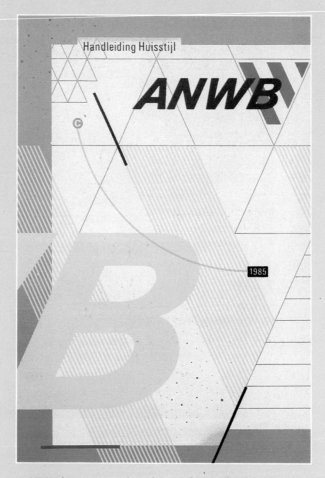

*NWB identity manual, Studio Dumbar, Holland, c.1984-5.*

# CHAPTER · SEVEN

# 1980
— TO —
# TODAY

# INTRODUCTION

After the ethic of the 1950s and 1960s (heavily influenced by Swiss design) which called for structure and discipline, a revolution began which brought a new era of freedom and expression in graphic design. It originated in the 1970s and appeared in a variety of forms, or movements. In America it was found in the movement called New Wave, Post Modern, Swiss Punk or a number of other names. In Europe, where labels are less common, it emanated from groups and individuals – all with their own influences and direction, but incorporating a new experimental approach in their work.

It would be a mistake to say that the new spirit was solely a rejection of 1950s and 1960s formalism, for many of the practitioners of the new expression incorporate formalist influences in their work – a sense of order, structure and precision are often highly detectable. However, there are also groups important to this era whose approach could only be described as anarchic, or based in the irrational. Although it had its roots in the 1970s, the new spirit – broadly termed the avant garde – consolidated itself and took a strong hold in the 1980s, infiltrating the most sober areas of graphic design (such as corporate programmes) and representing the most conservative of clients.

The avant garde recognizes the new themes and issues of the 1980s – instead of providing the barest of visual statements, it provides the fullest. Its statements can at times be intensely personal. Information is often put across amidst layers of imagery which provide contextual comments and additional thoughts (such as in the use of collage). Heavy use of photography and photomontage provides a strong sense of here and now – images of popular culture often override the old sense of craft evoked by the drawn image. The traditional drawn mark has been electrified and exploded beyond all recognition, and rigid compositional arrangements (so dear to Swiss design) have given way to painterly obsessions with colour, texture, layering. (When described in such terms, it hardly sounds like graphic design!) It commands a range of media that is bewilderingly broad, from the use of graphics computers to 'instant' media, such as photocopiers. Its imagery can be coarse and provocative, as well as refined and sensual. The *avant garde* spirit of the 1980s is out for individuality, imagination, emotion, shock effect – all the things that the systems and rationale of the previous decades couldn't offer.

It is not surprising that Holland features strongly in this era, for over the decades it has proved to be a progressive country in its social attitudes. Art and design hold important positions in Holland's overall scheme of values (as shown by the '1 per cent arrangement' – the government ruling whereby 1 per cent of the construction cost of public buildings is to be used to commission art). Historically it has always had an avant garde in the form of De Stijl, Theo van Doesburg, Piet Zwart and others, and today's Dutch de-

*Ministry of Education and Science house magazine, Frans Lieshout/Total Design, Holland, 1980s.*

signers can draw influences from Dada, the Bauhaus, Constructivism, Futurism, etc. This healthy smattering of influences has prevented total immersion in one or the other. Unlike America, for example, where the Swiss style was taken much more seriously and therefore left a rather heavy mark on the New Wave of the 1970s. Additionally, the high quality of Dutch printing does great justice to its experimental designers – an important asset which should not be overlooked. Many of the progressive works produced currently, especially for the ptt (Dutch Postal Services), also happen to be examples of exquisite printing.

Another matter of interest – the avant garde is generally associated with youth culture in Britain (i.e. age brings conservatism and common sense). However, in Holland and other countries, the avant garde spirit possesses a very mixed age grouping, and most of the people mentioned are definitely not 'youth'. It is also possible to form arguments about the boundaries of avant garde – who is and who isn't. The term is used broadly here and has only one implication – that of innovation.

## The Netherlands

The Netherlands' contribution to the avant garde is a powerful one. To describe its presence within the closely-knit Dutch design community is rather like telling the story of a family with wayward relations and offspring. There are differences of approach within the community to be sure. Some studios are intent on hanging on to their grids while the avant garde spirit grows and prospers around them. It has even been said that a competitive edge can now be detected between the rational groups based in Amsterdam and the avant garde groups based in The Hague. That doesn't however seem to stop them from collaborating on projects together! The Dutch graphic design community has also increased its size; the major groups of the 1970s have produced further splinter groups and solo designers relevant to the new spirit of the 1980s.

An important and highly respected figure to this scenario is R. D. E. (Ootje) Oxenaar, in his role as Head of the Art and Design Branch of the ptt (Dutch Postal Services) in The Hague. The Art and Design Branch is responsible for the use of the visual arts in ptt buildings, granting commissions to artists and purchasing works of art. It also commissions artists and designers for postage stamps and other printed material.

Through the Art and Design Branch, Oxenaar has acted as a source of encouragement and support for young designers and design studios over the past decade and has himself designed forms, stamps and other material. His most extraordinary piece of work, however, appears in that most ephemeral of graphic forms – money. Over a twenty year period (mid-1960s to the present day), Oxenaar has designed a set of banknotes for the Netherlands Bank which are modern in style, and full of beauty and invention. (Relief points enabling blind users to identify note values were used here for the first time.)

Following on from that, the avant garde spirit can best be pursued according to cities…beginning with Amsterdam. Total Design in Amsterdam, known since the 1960s for its highly rational Swiss design base, has occasionally shown signs of being influenced by the new spirit of freedom in graphics. But it is still regarded as the Dutch bastion of straightforward, systematic graphic design, and its more unconventional work over the years was often carried out by either Frans Lieshout or Anthon Beeke. Frans Lieshout is a current member of Total and his use of peculiar-shaped formats is immediately recognizable in Total's collection. This includes Total Design's 20th anniversary publication (an oblique-shaped book) and a nuclear disarmament poster trimmed at odd angles.

Anthon Beeke dropped out of art school in earlier years to become involved with Fluxus, a performance art group in Amsterdam. He then worked for Total Design (his work is also highly identifiable in their 20th anniversary group publication) and since 1981 has operated his own studio. He has been involved in a broad range of work and is perhaps best known for the posters he designed for the Globe Theatre company in Eindhoven (1977/84) which contain provocative and often disturbing imagery. In the mid-1980s he was commissioned for two ptt books, *Nederlandse Postzegels* (1985), which were concerned with stamps produced in 1980/81. Normally such books would provide an authoritative description of the stages and techniques involved in producing the stamps, from initial design concept to final printed result. Beeke's books however are a celebrated departure from the norm, incorporating imaginative and playful artistic statements. (One book contains a fantasy life-story of the travels and adventures of one stamp. The stamp concerned was issued by an imaginary tribal king, and bears his portrait…drawn with the features of Beeke himself!) Beeke teaches at the Gerrit Rietveld Academy in Amsterdam, as does a longer established member of the avant garde scene, Jan van Toorn.

Jan van Toorn, freelance graphic designer in Amsterdam, has been involved over the years in various movements concerning the role of art in society and much of his work has political and social overtones. He is particularly known for designing the annual calendar for the printing firm Mart Spruijt from 1960 to 1977. Van Toorn often constructed his calendar designs with pictures of ordinary people taken from newspapers and magazines, or collaged photos of world politicians into settings or situations which made overt political statements, extending the role of the calendar to that of a historical document.

He is also known for his long-term association with the Van Abbe Museum in Eindhoven. He designed many of its posters, catalogues and exhibitions, and was involved in the museum's continuing re-assessment of its role and function

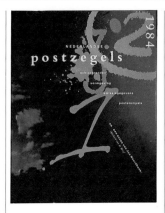

*Nederlande Postzegels books, Anthon Beeke for ptt, Holland, 1985.*

in society. Van Toorn's social commitment still continues, as shown in his 1985 posters for the De Beyerd museum in Breda, publicizing a series of exhibitions on the theme 'Man and the Environment'.

Concepts Design is a relatively recent addition to the Amsterdam scene. It started in 1983 with the joining together of seven partners, all of whom already had well-established careers of their own. Concepts now has eight partners and spans graphic design, product development, industrial design and public relations – and their philosophy demands that clients deal with individual partners as opposed to a central office. Each design problem and solution is considered to be unique, and they are against having a Concepts 'style'. Their tone is serious and realistic, and they could be viewed as providing healthy competition for Total Design, although they presently operate on a smaller scale. Like Total, they occasionally display an unconventional streak – such as in a range of

Studio Dumbar, launched in 1977 by Gert Dumbar, now enjoys an international reputation and is regarded as the centrepoint of Dutch avant garde graphics. Its earlier projects included the design of the well-known travelling exhibition on Dutch Design for the Public Sector and the adventurous Westeinde Hospital signage, incorporating a bouncing ball motif to identify each floor. The 1980s brought on the visual identity and signage for the Rijksmuseum in Amsterdam, and a plethora of stamps, letterheads and logos, book designs and covers, posters for museums, exhibitions and theatres and other projects. The broad range of work produced by Studio Dumbar is also essentially diverse in character, incorporating examples of sober and functional design as well as exuberant and free design.

posters for the Triad Stage Alliance in London.

Turning to the city of Den Haag, also known as The Hague, the spirit of the avant garde becomes stronger, freer, and acquires a tremendous sense of fun.

At the heart of Studio Dunbar lies an experimental attitude – challenging conventions, exploring new methods and techniques. In the work there is also an underlying presence of social concern, and an understanding of human emotional needs such as humour, beauty, irreverence and playfulness. The uniqueness of their work however lies in the dual (opposing) associations it so often carries: rational and irrational, serious and humorous.

Gert Dumbar has also been active and influential in design education, not only in Dutch schools but more recently as Professor of Graphic Art and Design at the Royal College of Art in London. The Studio itself functions as a communication link-up for the design education world. Students are employed on a short-term basis as part of the team at Studio Dumbar, coming from the Cranbrook

# INTRODUCTION

Academy in the USA, the Royal College of Art in Britain and favoured design schools in The Netherlands such as St Joost in Breda.

The Hague avant garde scene includes Vorm Vijf, a large established Studio of young designers which operates in friendly rivalry to Studio Dumbar. Also emanating from The Hague, and an important name for the future, is Ko Sliggers. He began his career at Studio Dumbar, then started working alone (now in Amsterdam) and is currently one of the most influential young designers in The Netherlands.

On to Rotterdam. Justly annoyed with the idea that all culture emanates from Amsterdam or The Hague, in 1978 the city of Rotterdam provided finance for a magazine about art in Rotterdam. The magazine was entitled *Hard Werken*, and the group of designers collaborating on it set up a design studio in parallel, also named Hard Werken. Ten issues of the magazine were produced and Hard Werken are now hailed among young people in The Netherlands as the most extreme of the avant garde groups, working mainly for the cultural sector – theatres, publishers, the arts. Their philosophy (roughly translated): 'Everything is done for no reason at all'.

## The United States

For the USA, the 1980s brought Ronald Reagan and an all-out Hollywood attempt at reviving national pride and putting America back on top of the world. Graphic design at this point is becoming a massive industry, women are more present in the profession than ever before, computer graphics technology is operating both in professional studios and in education (far more so than in Europe) and the styles and influences are still ranging over a broad spectrum, from folklore to space age. The so-called New Wave Movement which grew out of Swiss design and flourished in the 1970s has provided a couple of major stars for the 1980s (along with a cast of thousands, or even more).

On the West Coast April Greiman has applied her highly

*Down Hill Poster, from Print, US, 1983.*

developed sense of collage to posters, magazines and corporate identity programmes, and has extended even further into three-dimensional design with interiors and furniture. She also received formal Swiss graphic design training and a resulting preoccupation with structuring and order is clearly detectable in her work. But there is much more to it than that. Her work also shows an artistic obsession with colour and texture, and the concept of order in space. In Greiman's collages, spacial depth is achieved through many layers of varying visual elements – a two-dimensional plane is conceived as a three-dimensional experience. Her more recent work pursues these issues through use of an ideal medium, the Apple Macintosh computer.

An April Greiman project particularly worth noting is her recent design of a special edition of Design Quarterly magazine (no. 133), entitled 'Does it make sense?'. The entire issue unfolds to become a super-sized poster over six feet in length – a technical feat that is visually stunning as well.

## France

The design co-operative Grapus grew out of the climate surrounding the 1968 anti-establishment revolts in Paris, and similarly experienced in the UK, USA and Germany. Established values were being questioned, and hopes expressed for a new society. The visual language of this revolt came in the form of spontaneous posters appearing in Paris – mainly produced by non-professionals who felt strongly about the issues of the day.

Grapus was formed in 1970 by three communist graphic designers – Pierre Bernard, Francois Miehe, and Gerard Paris-Clavel. Their aim was to produce social, political and cultural images as a design co-operative and under a joint signature. They initially went to Poland to study graphic design under Henryk Tomaszewski, and on return to Paris set up their co-operative to carry on the spirit of 1968. They refused to undertake commercial projects or advertising, and would only work for progressive town councils, community centres, experimental theatres etc – causes which they considered worthwhile (and which seldom had funds). Their posters were a product of teamwork resulting from joint discussion, and were usually fly-posted at night over commercial billboards.

Their recent work is not confined to posters – they also produce letterheads, corporate identities, exhibitions and other projects. The size and membership of the team has changed over the years, but Grapus remain ever true to their objectives although constantly in debt (while winning many national and international prizes for their work).

Also in the 1960s, France acquired an exceptional emigrant from Poland. Roman Cieslewicz initially gained recognition in Poland for poster design in the late 1950s and early 1960s. He left Poland and emigrated to France in 1963,

---

Moving back towards the East Coast, Cranbrook Academy in Michigan provides another hotspot for the avant garde. A small postgraduate institution, the design department has been under the joint-chairmanship (husband and wife team) of Mike and Kathy McCoy since 1971. Kathy is the graphic design side of the team, with Mike on the products and interior side, and they work jointly (transferring concepts freely between 2-D and 3-D) and

separately. Kathy McCoy received her foundation in the Swiss tradition, but on arrival at Cranbrook experimentation opened new directions which she also transferred to the work of the department. Largely due to the McCoy influence, Cranbrook is recognized for its experimental approach to graphics and has also developed links with Europe. (Cranbrook students have worked at Studio Dumbar in The Netherlands, for example.)

and has been living and teaching in Paris since then. In the 1960s he was responsible for art direction in a number of Paris magazines such as *Elle* and *Vogue*, and became particularly known for poster design incorporating powerful photomontage imagery and often using greatly enlarged halftones. In the 1970s and 1980s, his posters and photomontage imagery have become increasingly surrealistic and bizarre, possessing a controlled and studied form of shock effect.

## Switzerland

Wolfgang Weingart's work and teaching has been regarded by many as the foundation of the 1970s New Wave Movement in America, and his influence is still strongly felt there in the 1980s. His typography projects at the Kunstgewerbeschule Basle are world renowned, and although the classes there originally dealt exclusively with hand-composed metal type and letterpress printing, they have developed over the years to encompass new media techniques (such as film collage) and, in the 1980s, experimentation with the Apple Macintosh computer.

Since 1972 he has lectured throughout Europe and the United States (at various institutions such as Yale University, Princeton University, California Institute of the Arts) and more recently has also conducted typography workshops at the Yale University Summer Program in Graphic Design/Brissago, Switzerland. But the strongest cross-Atlantic link is still the Basle school, for American students working with Weingart at Basle (and European students, for that matter) return home and, often becoming teachers themselves, spread his ideas and methods while continually adding their own. Although the ideas change and develop as the chain grows, happily the original sense of experimentation and freedom remains intact and transfers down the line.

## Germany

Similar to Grapus in France, the German graphic design studio of Rambow Lienemeyer van de Sand (a team of three) emerged in the aftermath of political motivation and social conscience in the 1970s, but is best set in the progressive spirit of the 1980s.

Their work is characterized by a heavy sense of surrealism achieved through use of photography and photomontage. The message and the effect, however, is always hard-hitting and direct and it is this quality that makes their work distinctive with their visual language often acting as a tool for social comment.

*Octavo 86, typography journal, 8vo, Britain, 1986.*

## Britain

In the early 1980s, small young graphic design groups were cropping up in London faster than lightning – by the mid-1980s the same could be said for animation companies. Pop promos and television commercial advertising are boom industries, particularly with regard to computer animation. Advances already include the creation of the TV character Max Headroom in 1985 by Annabel Jankel and Rocky Morton. However, the field is still growing rapidly and promises an exciting future in Britain.

Innovations in graphic design are mainly to be found in magazines aimed at pop culture. *i-D* magazine was originally a fashion fanzine launched in 1980 by Terry Jones (editor, art director and co-publisher) which hyped ordinary clothes/people in the street as Fashion – a street-style catalogue, and certainly a by-product of punk. Employing a design ethic of arbitrary clutter produced by instant methods (random type styles, photocopier distortions, any-old-letraset to hand) it has aged fairly well and in the mid-1980s still retains some of its original recklessness.

*The Face* magazine also appeared in 1980, aimed at the youth market. It covered art, design, music and fashion, and received stylishly radical art direction from Neville Brody. *The Face* introduced a new approach to fashion photography in Britain, often sacrificing a proper view of the garments in order to project atmosphere, attitudes and lifestyles.

British advertising is still as strong as ever: examples include the 1984/85 'Say No to No Say' campaign against the abolition of the Greater London Council by London ad agency Boase Massimi Pollitt; and recently on billboards The Colours of Benetton – a double-meaning in the headlines, celebrating the colours of Benetton's clothing collections as well as the colours of the multi-racial consumers.

Rebel activities can also be mentioned in two other areas. Rising out of a frustration with mainstream design education, in 1985 the independent School of Communication Arts was launched in London with John Gillard as its Head and financial backing from design and advertising studios. Also 'artists books' (using the book as an art form in itself), private press and general lone-wolf publishing (from groups such as Octavo and Coracle) experience a rise in popularity – important alternatives in a country where the mainstream publishing industry has suffered financial setbacks over the past decade and is consequently unwilling to take risks.

# POSTERS

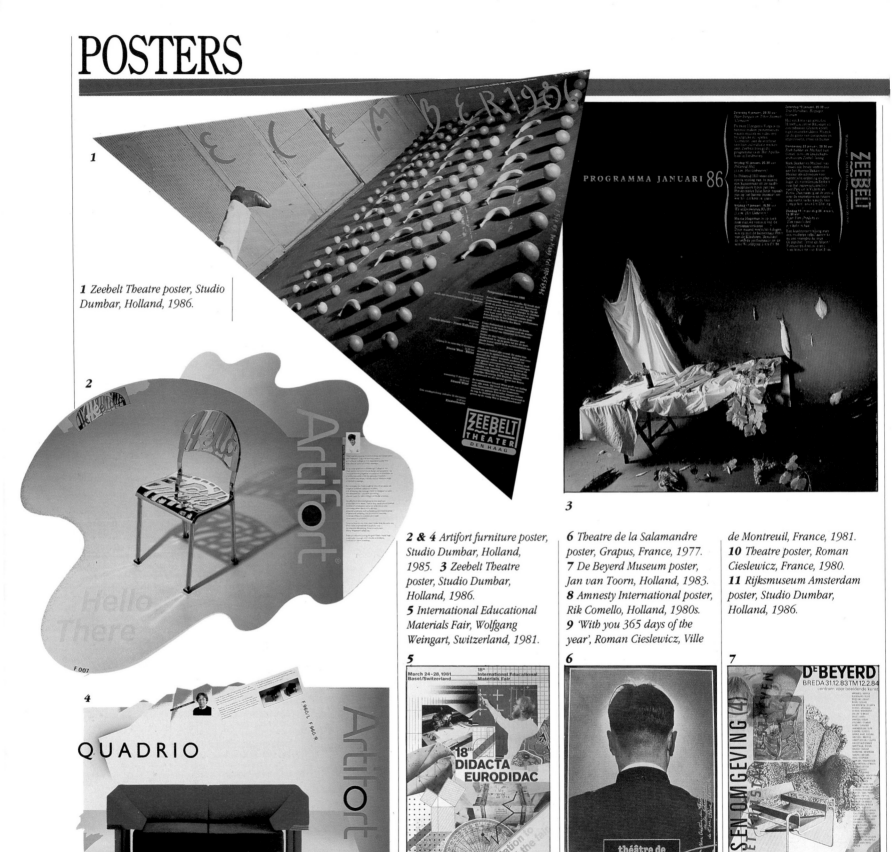

1 Zeebelt Theatre poster, Studio Dumbar, Holland, 1986.

2 & 4 Artifort furniture poster, Studio Dumbar, Holland, 1985. 3 Zeebelt Theatre poster, Studio Dumbar, Holland, 1986.
5 International Educational Materials Fair, Wolfgang Weingart, Switzerland, 1981.

6 Theatre de la Salamandre poster, Grapus, France, 1977.
7 De Beyerd Museum poster, Jan van Toorn, Holland, 1983.
8 Amnesty International poster, Rik Comello, Holland, 1980s.
9 'With you 365 days of the year', Roman Cieslewicz, Ville

de Montreuil, France, 1981.
10 Theatre poster, Roman Cieslewicz, France, 1980.
11 Rijksmuseum Amsterdam poster, Studio Dumbar, Holland, 1986.

180

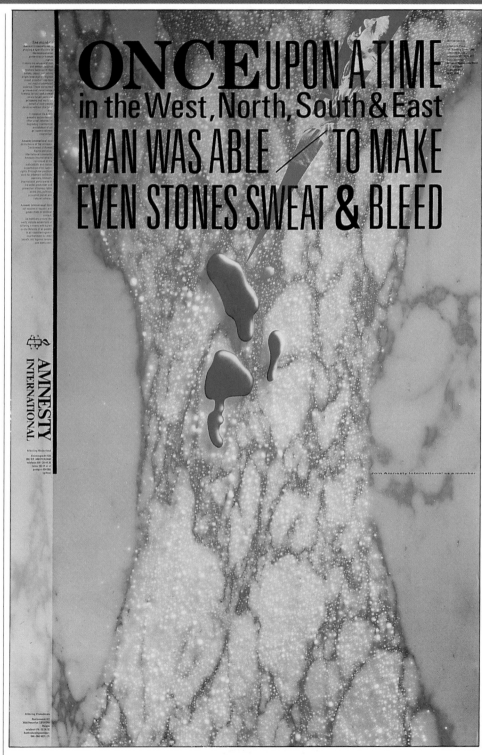

**8**

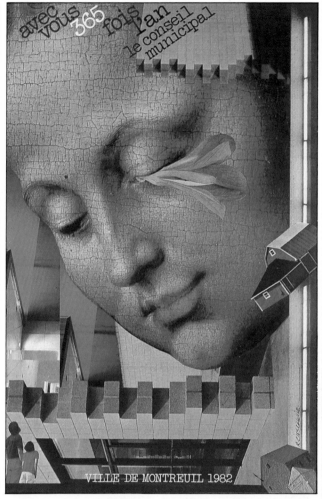

VILLE DE MONTREUIL 1982

**9**

roman cieślewicz

**10**

Kunst voor de beeldenstorm

Noordnederlandse kunst 1525-1580

**11**

# POSTERS

**1**

**2**

**3**

**4**

**5**

**1** *The New American Home, poster for Builder magazine, US, 1975.* **2** *Vorm Vijf poster, Vorm Vijf, Holland, 1984.* **3** *Gevrey Chambertin poster, Grapus, France, 1982.*

**4** *Hacienda nightclub, 4th birthday poster, 8vo, Britain, 1986.* **5** *Sequences — InformationTexture, April Grieman, US, 1985.* **6** *Largo Desolato, Hans Bockting/ Concepts, Holland, 1986.*

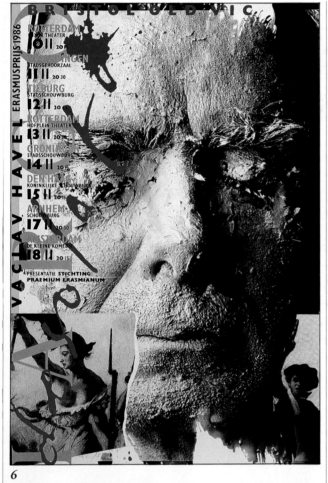

6

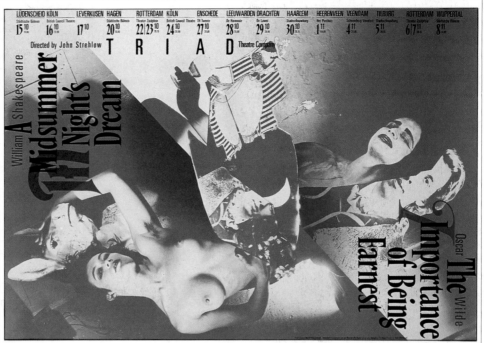

7

**7** *Triad Theatre Company poster, Hans Bockting/ Concepts, Holland 1980s.*
**8** *Festival Poster, Hard Werken, Holland, 1983.* **9** *Amadeus, Roman Cieslewicz, France, 1982.* **10** *Les Cenci, Grapus, France, 1981.*
**11** *Rijksmuseum Amsterdam poster, Studio Dumbar, 1986.*

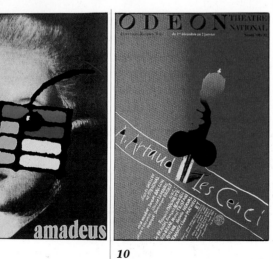

9

10

8

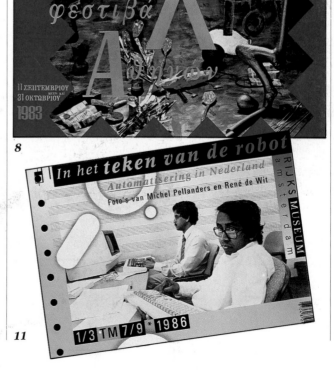

11

# MAGAZINES

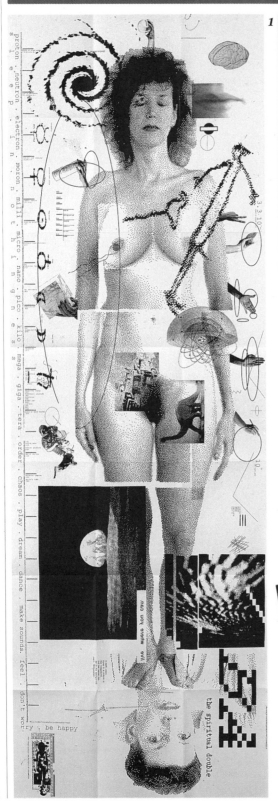

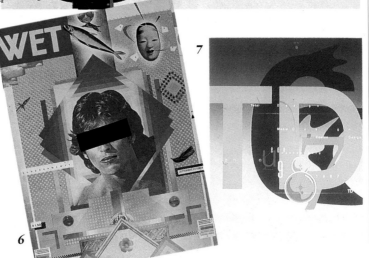

**1** *Design Quarterly 133, poster, April Greiman, US, 1986.*
**2** *Technology Review, art director Nancy Cahners, US, 1983.* **3, 5 & 8** *Macobouw brochure, Frans Lieshout/Total Design, Holland, 1987.*
**4** *Spread from Print, US, 1983.*

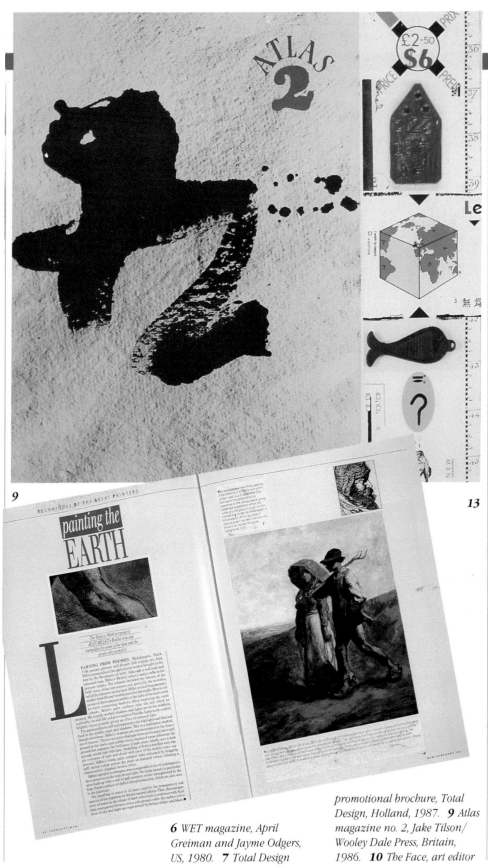

9

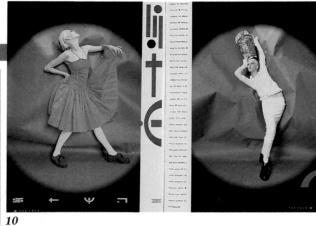

10

11

12

13

14

**6** WET magazine, April
Greiman and Jayme Odgers,
US, 1980.  **7** Total Design
promotional brochure, Total
Design, Holland, 1987.  **9** Atlas
magazine no. 2, Jake Tilson/
Wooley Dale Press, Britain,
1986.  **10** The Face, art editor
Neville Brody, Britain, August
1984.  **11** The Face, art editor
Neville Brody, Britain, January
1985.  **12** i-D Magazine, art
director Terry Jones, Britain,
September 1986.  **13** Spread
from the Artist and Illustrator
magazine, art editor Caroline
Grimshaw, February 1987.
**14** i-D magazine, art editor
Moira Bogue, Britain,
November 1985.

# INFORMATION DESIGN

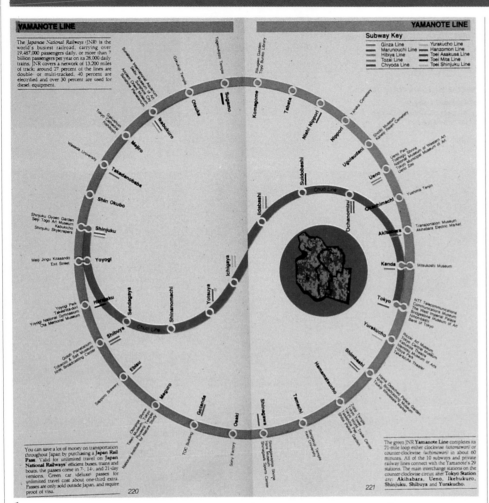

1 *Guide to Tokyo, Richard Saul Wurman, Graphis Annual, 1985-86.* 2 *Which? magazine, shopfitting logos, Grundy Northedge, Britain, 1980s.* 3 *Lambton Place studios, logo for public information publications 'Minding your* own business', Grundy Northedge, Britain, 1980s. 4 *Diagram showing population by country, Britain 1981,* Grundy Northedge, Britain. 5 *TIME magazine chart, Nigel Holmes, US.* 6 *Page from TIME magazine, Nigel Holmes, US.*

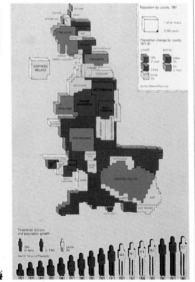

# TYPOGRAPHY

1 *Spread from Europa Joieria Contemporania, exhibition catalogue, Fundacio Caixa de Pensions, Barcelona, 1987.*
2 *Invitation, Rubin Cordaro, Design, US, 1983.* 3 *Heinz Ketchup typography study model, Kathy McCoy and Robert Nakata, Cranbrook Academy of Art, US, 1980s.*

**1**

**2**

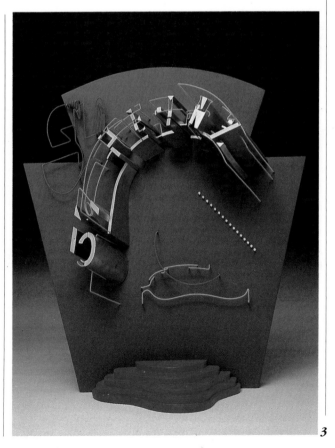

**3**

# INDEX

# INDEX

# CREDITS

**p10**, *1* Giraudon © ADAGP, 1987. **pp12-13**, *1* Bridgeman Art Library © DACS, 1987. *2* Design Council © DACS, 1987. *3* By courtesy of the Board of Trustees of the Victoria and Albert Museum © DACS, 1987. *4* Museum of Modern Art, New York. **pp14-15**, *3* By courtesy of the Board of Trustees of the Victoria and Albert Museum. **pp16-17**, *1* ET Archive. **pp18-19**, *1-7* Robert Opie Collection. **pp20-21**, *1-2* Robert Opie Collection. *3-8* Retrograph Archive Collection. *9-10* Robert Opie Collection. *11* Retrograph Archive Collection. *12-13* Robert Opie Collection. **pp22-23**, *1-28* Robert Opie Collection. **pp24-25**, *1* Peter Newark's Western Americana. *2* Retrograph Archive Collection. *3-4* Peter Newark's Western Americana. *5* David King Collection. *6-7* Peter Newark's Western Americana. **pp26-27**, *1-4* Lords Gallery. *5* Lords Gallery © ADAGP, 1987. *6-7* Robert Opie Collection. *8* Trustees of the Imperial War Museum © DACS, 1987. *9-10* Lords Gallery. *11* Lords Gallery © ADAGP, 1987. **pp28-29**, *1* Robert Opie Collection. *2* Trustees of the Imperial War Museum. *3* Robert Opie Collection. *4* Bridgeman Art Library. *5* Robert Opie Collection. *6* Trustees of the Imperial War Museum. *7* Peter Newark's Western Americana. *8* Trustees of the Imperial War Museum. *9* Trustees of the Imperial War Museum © DACS, 1987. **pp30-31**, *1*David King Collection. *2* VEB Verlag der Kunst, Dresden © DACS, 1987. *3* Lords Gallery © Cosmopress, Geneva and DACS, London, 1987. *4* David King Collection. *5-6* Retrograph Archive Collection. *7* David King Collection © DACS, 1987. **p32**, *1* David King Collection. *5* By courtesy of the Board of Trustees of the Victoria and Albert Museum. *6-7* David King Collection. *10* The Daily Mirror. **p34**, *1-2* Design Council © DACS, 1987. *4 & 7* Graphic Trade Symbols by German Designers, Dover Publications Inc. **p38**, London Regional Transport. **p39**, *1-3* Colin Narbeth. **p40**, Retrograph Archive Collection. **p44**, *1* Retrograph Archive Collection. *2* Robert Opie Collection. **p45**,*6* ET Archive. **pp46-47**, *1-2* Robert Opie Collection. *3* Milner Gray. *4-6* Robert Opie Collection. **pp48-49**, *1* Retrograph Archive Collection *2-8* Robert Opie Collection. **pp50-51**, *1-5* Robert Opie Collection. *6* Peter Newark's Western

Americana. **pp52-53**, *1* Shell U.K. Ltd. *2* Robert Opie Collection. *3* The Trustees of the Imperial War Museum. *4* Lords Gallery © DACS, 1987. **pp54-55**, *1* David King Collection. *2* Lords Gallery © ADAGP, 1987. *3* ET Archive/RAF Museum, Hendon. *4* Lords Gallery © ADAGP, 1987. *5* Lords Gallery. *6* The Trustees of the Imperial War Museum © ADAGP, 1987. *7* The Trustees of the Imperial War Museum. **pp56-57**, *1* Retrograph Archive Collection. *2* Hulton Picture Library/Syndication International. *4* Retrograph Archive Collection/ Condé Nast. *5* Design Council. *6* Robert Opie Collection. *7* Retrograph Archive Collection. *8* Robert Opie Collection. **pp58-59**, *1-2* Penguin Group. *3* David King Collection. *5* David King Collection *7* By courtesy of the Board of Trustees of the Victoria and Albert Museum. *9-12* Academy Editions. **pp60-61**, *1* The Trustees of the Imperial War Museum. *2* Design Council. *3* Peter Newark's Western Americana. *5-6* London Regional Transport. **p64**, *3* Simpson's. **p65**, *1-5* The Post Office. **p66**, The Post Office. **p68-69**, *1* Museum of Modern Art, New York. *2* The Trustees of the Imperial War Museum. **pp70-71**, *1 & 3* The Trustees of the Imperial War Museum. *2* The Trustees of the Imperial War Museum © DACS, 1987. **p72**, *1, 2 & 5* Retrograph Archive Collection. **p73**, *1-3 & 5-6* Retrograph Archive Collection. **p74**, *1-7* The Trustees of the Imperial War Museum. *4* The Trustees of the Imperial War Museum © DACS, 1987. *5* The Trustees of the Imperial War Museum © DACS, 1987. **p75**, *1-3* The Trustees of the Imperial War Museum © DACS, 1987. *4* Design Council. *5-11* The Trustees of the Imperial War Museum. **pp78-79**, *5-6* Retrograph Archive Collection/ Condé Nast. **p80**, *5* Curtis Publishing Co. **p82**, *1* Collins. *2-4* Penguin Group. **p83**, *1* Paul Rand. *6* Design Council. **pp84-85**, *1* Times Newspapers. *2* The Daily Telegraph. **p86**, *1* The Trustees of the Imperial War Museum. **p87**, *1-4* Colin Narbeth. **pp90-91**, *1* Paul Rand. **pp92-93**, *1* Penguin Group. *2-3* The Post Office. *4* Design Council/ Design Research Unit. **pp94-95**, *2 & 4* Retrograph Archive Collection. *7* Design Council. **96-97**, *7* Retrograph Archive Collection. **pp100-101**, *1*

Retrograph Archive Collection. *4* © DACS, 1987. *9* Peter Newark's Western Americana. *10* CBS. **pp102-103**, *1* Museum of Modern Art, New York © DACS, 1987. *2* British Film Institute. *4* British Film Institute. *5* Design Council *6* Design Council/ Olivetti SpA, Milan. *7* Robert Opie Collection. *8* Verlag Arthur Niggli, Switzerland. **p104**, *2* Verlag Arthur Niggli, Switzerland. *1-2* Penguin Group. *3-4* Pan Books. **p105**, *1-3* Esquire Inc. *4* Ideal Home. *5* Hulton Picture Library/Syndication International. *7-8* Crowel-Collier Publishing Co. **p106**, *5-6* McCalls. **p108**, *1* Verlag Arthur Niggli, Switzerland. *2* Capitol Records. *4* Philips Ltd. *5* CBS Records. *6* Decca Records. **p109**, *1* ET Archive. *5* CBS. *6* Design Council. **p112**,*1-4* Colin Narbeth. **p112**, The Daily Express. **p114-115**, *1* Doyle Dane Bernbach Ltd. *2* Bodleian Library/Conservative Central Office. **pp116-117**, *1* Design Council. *2* Roman Cieslewicz. **p118**, *1* Design Council. **pp120-121**, *2-5* Robert Opie Collection. **pp122-123**, *1* Peter Newark's Western Americana. *4* Olivetti SpA, Milan. *5-7* Doyle Dane Bernbach Ltd. **pp124-125**, *1* The Trustees of the Imperial War Museum. **p126**, *1* Verlag Arthur Niggli, Switzerland. *3 & 5* By courtesy of the Board of Trustees of the Victoria and Albert Museum. *6* Wim Crouwel/Total Design. **p129**, *1-2* The Sunday Times. *3* © DACS, 1987. **p131**, *1-4* Guido Pressler Verlag, Germany. **p132**, *3* Paul Hamlyn Ltd. *4-5* Thames and Hudson Ltd. *6* Jonathan Cape Ltd. **p134-135**, *1-2* EMI Records. *4* CBS Records. **pp136-137**, *1* Design Council. *2-3* F.H.K. Henrion. *4* Banks & Miles. *5* F.H.K. Henrion. *6* Presse und Informationsamt des Landes Berlin *7* Paul Rand. *9* Rosmarie Tissi. *10* Design Council. **pp138-139**, *1-4* Büchergilde Gutenberg. *5* Design Council. *6-8* Bruce Robertson, Diagram Visual Information Ltd. **p141**, *3* Colin Narbeth. *5-8* The Post Office. **p144-145**, *1* Design Council. *2* Pentagram. **pp146-147**, *1* Lund Humphries. *2* Royal College of Art. *3* Stadtlsuyl Allgau. *4* Wolfgang Weingart. **pp148-149**, *1-8* Robert Opie Collection. *9* Pentagram. **pp150-151**,*1* Volvo. *2 & 4* Colt International. *3* Parker Pen Ltd. *5-9* Health Education Council. *6* Volkswagen. *7* Bankers Trust Company. *8* Newsweek International. **pp152-153**, *1* Wim Crouwel/Total

Design. *2* Gert Dunbar, Studio Dunbar. *3-4* F.H.K. Henrion © DACS, 1987. *5* Pentagram. *7* Roman Cieslewicz. **pp154-155**, *1, 2 & 4* Esquire Inc. *3 & 5* Hard Werken. *6* i-D Magazine. **pp156-157**,*1* i-D Magazine. *2 & 6* Typografische Monatsblätter/Wolfgang Weingart. *3* Wolfgang Weingart. *8-10* April Greiman and Jayme Odgers. **p158**, *1* Habitat Ltd. **159**, *1-6* Felix Gluck Publishing. **pp160-161**, *1* Virgin Records. *2* Atlantic Records. *3* ABC Records. *4* RCA Records. **pp162-163**, *1* Mueller Enterprise Inc. *2* Continental Airlines. *3* Alitalia. *4* Royal Bank of Scotland. *5* American Telephone & Telegraph. *6* International Wool Secretariat. *7* ELAL *9* Robert Leicht Brewery. *10* Barkon Petroleum Inc. *11* Liberty National Bank & Trust Company. *12* Cotton Inc. *13* Pan Am. *14* Parker Adult Games. *15* Quaker Oats Company. *16* AMF. *17* KLM Airlines. *20* Exxon. *21* Pepsi-Cola Company. *23* Levi Strauss Company. *24* General Telephone & Electronics. *25* Peter Newark's Western Americana. *28* Green Giant Company. *29* Design Research Unit. **pp164-5**, *1 & 2* QED. *5* The Diagram Group. **pp166-167**, *1* The Diagram Group. *2* QED. *3* QED. *4-7* Studio Dunbar. **pp168-169**, *1* Jan van Toorn. *5* National Consumer Council. **p171**, *6-9* © ADAGP, 1987. **pp172-173**, *1-3 & 8* The Post Office. *4-7* Jan van Toorn. *10* Studio Dunbar. **p174**, *1* Studio Dunbar. **pp176-177**, *1* Kathy McCoy. *2* Print. *3* 8vo. **pp180-181**, *1-4* Studio Dunbar. *5* Wolfgang Weingart. *6* Grapus. *7* Jan van Toorn. *8* Rik Comello. *9-10* Roman Cieslewicz. *11* Studio Dunbar. **pp182-183**, *1* Vorm Vijf. *3* Grapus. *4* 8vo. *5* April Greiman. *6-7* Hans Bockting/Concepts. *8* Hard Werken. *9* Roman Cieslewicz. *10* Grapus. *11* Studio Dunbar. **pp184-185**, *1* April Greiman. *3, 5 & 8* Frans Lieshout/ Total Design. *4* Print, New York. *6* April Greiman and Jayme Odgers. *7* Total Design. *9* Atlas/Woolley Dale Press. *10-11* The Face/Wagadon Ltd. *12 & 14* i-D Magazine. *13* Quarto Publishing. **p186**, *2-4* Grundy Northedge. *5-6* Nigel Holmes. **p187**, *2* Print, New York. *3* Kathy McCoy.

Every effort has been made to trace and acknowledge all copyright holders. Quarto would like to apologise if any omissions have been made.